The Making of a Man

(and why we're so afraid to talk about it)

OBIOMA UGOALA

SCRIBNER

LONDON NEW YORK SYDNEY TORONTO NEW DELHI

First published as *The Problem With My Normal Penis*
First published in Great Britain by Scribner,
an imprint of Simon & Schuster UK Ltd, 2022
This edition published in 2023

1 3 5 7 9 10 8 6 4 2

Simon & Schuster UK Ltd
1st Floor
222 Gray's Inn Road
London WC1X 8HB

Simon & Schuster Australia, Sydney
Simon & Schuster India, New Delhi

www.simonandschuster.co.uk
www.simonandschuster.com.au
www.simonandschuster.co.in

A CIP catalogue record for this book
is available from the British Library

Paperback ISBN: 978-1-3985-0481-3
eBook ISBN: 978-1-3985-0480-6

Typeset in Palatino by M Rules
Printed and Bound in the UK using 100% Renewable
Electricity at CPI Group (UK) Ltd

To Dartagnan, E and C.
You are the reason I pour myself out and leave myself empty.
May you always try to pass the ladder back down.

A NOTE TO THE READER

At the core of this book are the experiences that have formed, broken and moulded me into the man I am today. Some of these were traumatic for me but may also be potentially triggering to read (there are for instance homophobic slurs that are recounted in 'The Malunion of a Fracture'). I would urge the reader to take caution if reading them may cause distress.

CONTENTS

Preface

'Tis but thy name that is my enemy:
Thou art thyself, though not a Montague.
What's Montague? It is nor hand nor foot
Nor arm nor face nor any other part
Belonging to a man. O be some other name.
What's in a name? That which we call a rose
By any other name would smell as sweet;

From *Romeo and Juliet*, Act II, Scene II

I hate introductions. No matter how many times I introduce myself or somebody takes that burden on for me, an overwhelming sense of self-consciousness washes over me as my brain becomes a disaster-scenario simulator with super computer processing capabilities. How do I look? This person looks familiar – have we met before or are they just another performer you've watched and are a fan of? What are you doing with your hands? You've had these for decades now – why don't you know what to do with them as you're saying your name? Should you make a joke about saying your name? 'Obi, like "Obi-Wan Kenobi"'? Wait, what's their name? What's in a name indeed, Mr Shakespeare.

When I first thought about writing this book, the title was the part that initially came to me.

'The Problem with my N***** Penis'.

If you have grown up in the West, when you see 'N' followed by five asterisks, you have been socialised to have certain expectations as to what is being obscured. There is a typical, or *normal*, response to those asterisks. It seemed to me a distillation of the central argument of my book.

'The Problem with my *Normal* Penis'.

It was the way in which I wanted to introduce my book to the world. I *wanted* potential readers to judge my book by its cover and, in doing so, think about how they had come to that judgement. As a Black man growing up in Britain, I had become increasingly aware of the way I had been socialised as a man and racialised as Black. The provocation of the title was to challenge my reader to interrogate what they thought of as *normal* and how much they left notions of race, sex and masculinity unexamined and taken for granted. What assumptions did my reader make about what *normal* is and how unconsciously had they arrived at those assumptions? Maya Angelou once said, 'Do the best you can until you

2

know better. Then when you know better, do better.' The gauntlet I felt I should throw down to my readers was to do better, to confront what they thought of as 'normal'. But how many of us can honestly say that they typically respond positively to confrontation? Little did I know that the 'provocative' element of my title would not be my playing with the heuristic of the N-word, but rather something more prudish and, ultimately, alarming.

In the process of promoting the book, I would find myself invited on to several radio shows by producers who had read early proofs and found the content to be urgent, necessary and important. Yet, inevitably, each of these appearances would be prefaced with variations of the statement, 'If you could just do us a favour and not mention the title of your book too often, as it's a morning show. We don't want any complaints from Ofcom.' The inability to name the 'part belonging to a man' would prove detrimental, handcuffed as the interviewer and I would be, treading on eggshells. How do you promote something that you cannot name? But it wasn't just in radio appearances. Friends who would ask for the book in high-street stores reported bashful and bemused looks from booksellers, while both parties lowered their voices as if discussing some scandalous, banned text à la D. H. Lawrence. If we are too embarrassed to even name the component parts of masculinity that intersect with race and sexuality, how can we ever truly hope to effect real change?

On 30 September 2021, serving police officer Wayne Couzens was sentenced to life imprisonment for the murder of Sarah Everard after using his position as a police officer to abduct and later kill the thirty-three-year-old woman. In the USA, on 20 April 2021, Derek Chauvin was found guilty of the murder of George Floyd after what the Minneapolis Police Department initially described as a 'medical incident during police interaction'. Both of these cases attracted huge public attention and outcry as these names became synonymous with the deep level of racism and misogyny that permeated British and American culture. Reforms were promised, inquiries launched and institutional self-reflection pledged. Yet for campaigners for racial justice and against gender violence both in Britain and in the United States, there is a familiar feeling of stagnation and inertia.

On both sides of the Atlantic, the phrase 'a few bad apples' has been employed where the malpractice of a few should not be seen as representative of the larger group, thus negating the need for any large-scale reform. Yet the original idiom is 'a rotten apple quickly infects its neighbour'. By allowing ourselves to focus on these few, select examples, were we excusing the low-level rot that was infecting fellow police officers and our wider political discourse? In naming these few examples, did it excuse the necessity for perhaps more awkward and ultimately more essential self-reflection on how we have all come to learn about what gender, race and sexuality?

As I was interviewing community organiser Thomas Chigbo for this book, he said that most challenges can be approached in three questions: 'What? So what? Now what?'

For my part, my 'What?' was my discomfort with how I felt I had been socialised and raised in British society firstly as a man, and secondly how I had been racialised as Black, and how these two things intersected. So what? Well, so much of that socialising had happened on a subconscious level from those around me, who I am sure didn't mean any intentional harm and had inherited their own baggage about what to expect from a young Black man. It was only decades later that I began to question the damaging effects of raising a generation of children to perform gendered roles and accept racialised narratives, some of which had roots centuries old. Was I comfortable with my niece and nephew, my younger brother, my own potential future children being raised in a society that I hadn't tried my utmost to safeguard them from? How much hurt had I unintentionally caused and how could I expect anything to change if I wasn't willing to accept my own responsibility for that? Okay, but now what? What comes next? Did my confrontational title provoke a tidal wave of compassion and understanding? Did it give people permission to change their minds?

During the 'Twixmas of 2022 (fondly known in our family as 'the merrineum'), I found myself lounging in my parents' living room, overstuffed with Christmas leftovers and unsure how many days exactly it was until New Year's Eve. I was lazily thumbing the bookshelf when I found an old edition of John Steinbeck's *Of Mice and Men*, which I hadn't looked at since secondary school. I was but a few pages into the introduction when I read this: 'Try to understand men.

If you understand each other you will be kind to each other. Knowing a man well never leads to hate and almost always leads to love.' For days, those words stuck with me. What was my hope in writing this book? To start a confrontation or a conversation? If I genuinely wanted to understand and be understood, was the best way of doing it with a title that would cause them to retreat into bashfulness? Or did that only serve to shame them into coyness, with a cover that would cause embarrassment if read on public transport? I thought back to the hushed tones of booksellers, to the wary comments of radio producers and the noticeable shift at dinner parties when I would announce the title of my recently published book. Would I let the hubris of maintaining my original title hamstring my attempt to create a better world for those I care about to grow up in? Before I could ask other people to potentially change their own perspective, I might have to humble myself in recognising what I could also change. The success of humanity as a species has been our ability to cohere as a society, compromising with and learning from each other. All of that starts with a conversation. As the saying goes, 'If you want to go fast, go alone; if you want to go far, go together.' And we still have so much further to go.

So, without further ado, let's talk.

My name is Obioma Ugoala, and this is my book:

The Making of a Man: And Why We're So Afraid to Talk About It

1

The Malunion of a Fracture

*In a malunion, a bone heals but not in the right
position. You may have never had treatment for
the broken bone. Or, if you did have treatment, the
bone moved before it healed. Malunion symptoms
include constant pain long after treatment. If
severe enough, the condition can cause a deformity
and may require surgery to repair or correct it.*

University of Pittsburgh Medical Center

Home is where the heart is. Or so the saying goes. For as long
as I can remember, my heart has always been in music –
specifically singing. Whether it was harmonising with my
father as he led the music at Midnight Mass or the Motown
hits that we would sing along to on the long family drives
across Ireland, music has been my happy place. As luck, or

perhaps parental wisdom, would have it, the state Catholic boys' school in Fulham I attended between the ages of seven and eighteen had an enviable music programme. Whatever dislocation my older brothers and I felt about being some of the only students of Black heritage in a predominantly white school was offset by the opportunities it would yield, especially for a young boy obsessed with music. We had a choir that would go on to record soundtracks for *The Lord of the Rings* and *Sleepy Hollow*. Yet I was almost comically larger than my classmates, a feature that proved beneficial to my schoolboy rugby career. I was, according to several of my teachers, 'the first face they saw' when I was singled out for punishment in a noisy classroom on countless occasions.

Except for the music department. Throughout my eleven years at the school, the department would be an oasis; a place where I would be nurtured, challenged and have the horizons of my burgeoning musical obsession broadened. Before long, the aural satisfaction of the harmonies of a Mozart Mass rivalled the relish of the most crunching tackle on a rugby pitch. My various choirmasters and rugby coaches recognised that, despite my other teenage shortcomings, I could sing *and* I was a threat on the rugby pitch. In those moments, whether sacking a scrum-half or nailing a descant line, the fact I was one of the students of Black heritage in a predominantly white environment rarely seemed to matter. Only very rarely.

Sitting in my music class one day, aged eleven, the teacher announced to the class that this half-term we would be studying African drumming. My father had always been at pains to point out that Africa is not a country, and to be wary of people who use monolithic descriptions about the continent, but this was music class; there was nothing to worry about. My teacher, after handing out his worksheets, came to the front of the class and said that sometimes drumming was used as a form of communication in Africa. He then tapped out a rhythm on the lid of the piano at the front of the classroom and turned to me as the only Black student and asked me to translate.

The whole class turned round to look at me.

I looked back at the teacher, puzzled and a bit confused. But music is what made me special. Perhaps being Black is what makes me special too. There was nothing to be wary about here. My friends and teacher were waiting for what felt like forever. I paused. I sighed. 'Yes, I'm doing fine today. How are you, sir?'

The class howled with laughter. I did too. This was my home and the music department was like family. Family always laugh at each other. Family always laugh with each other. Our music classrooms often resembled the oversized New York apartments of the sitcom *Friends*, with the recurring cast of other members of the department consistently drifting in and out of our lessons if they had a free period under the pretence of grabbing some sheet music or extra hymnals. During these cameo appearances, as the teachers gossiped together, they would grab my attention, drum a rhythm on the grand piano and await my response. Each day I would pause, deciding if this would be the day that I would resist. But they were smiling. So were my classmates. This was funny. It was an in-joke between friends and mentors. Everyone makes jokes at home that outsiders wouldn't really get. And as long as you're in on the joke, then it stays funny. You can't be hurt. Who could really blame my thirty-year-old music teachers for joining in on the joke? These teachers, who would go on to nurture my gift and help me break into rooms I wouldn't *traditionally* be allowed in, were just teaching me the value of my uniqueness. In that classroom I would learn more than once that my Blackness held a narrow, hilarious value. The fact that my value was rooted in a gross stereotype of 'Africans having a natural sense of rhythm' would leave me conflicted. But, I thought to myself, even the happiest of homes isn't free from sadness.

There is a verse in scripture that is often cited by both sides of the debate when it comes to children and the disciplining of them: 'Foolishness is bound in the heart of a child; but the rod of correction shall drive it far from him' – Proverbs 22:15.

As much as my faith has gone through peaks and troughs over the past three decades, I've always felt that religious texts often make very astute observations about human nature. Children, like anybody trying to muddle their way through this messy thing called life, learn what to do and what not to do through 'the rod of correction'. For my part, I found my teachers demonstrated a startling lack of imagination in understanding the power that words had to cause harm and restrict the actions of those to whom they were directed. So, potential damage caused by these 'rods of correction' went unchecked, especially when employed by children in the classroom. More than once, in an effort to temper my response in the playground to teasing comments, my teachers would tell me to remember the mantra: *Sticks and stones may break my bones, but words will never hurt me.*

As an adult, I now understand the impulse behind the sentiment – one that my parents echoed. It was a hope that I would put my faith in my teachers; that I would rely on those in a position of authority to handle situations and ensure that I never acted on the urge to take matters into my own hands, no matter what words were thrown at me. As the father of three boys of African heritage (my youngest brother having not yet been born) who had always been big for their age, and taking his own experiences into account, my dad was well aware of the outsized attention I might receive from teachers. Intellectually understanding that I would have to learn to cultivate a thick skin at school was one thing; pretending that words had lost their power as 'rods' to beat me into shape was another.

As much as I enjoyed learning and singing the classical choral Mass settings of Mozart and Haydn that we endlessly rehearsed in the choir, my musical obsessions were with the more modern premier R&B and soul vocalists whose virtuosic technique and prowess I felt matched that of any operatic tenor or concert soprano. After my voice broke, I belatedly discovered Donny Hathaway and Marvin Gaye, and tried to emulate the vocal stylings of Sam Cooke and Brian McKnight. But during the '90s, before my voice had broken, my heart belonged to the leading female vocalists of the day, in particular Ms Whitney Houston and Ms Mariah Carey. It was my idolising of these two divas that would lead to one of my first fights at school.

When my mother finally relented to my persistent requests to buy #1's, she could never have anticipated the degree to which that Mariah Carey album would be overplayed in my bedroom. So word-perfect and overenthusiastic was I that *a cappella* renditions of the first half of the album would often be heard in the playground during lunch breaks or in corridors before music class. Although I have never shied away from drawing attention, I found myself frustrated by the limits of duetting with Mariah in my bedroom or having to sing *a cappella*. That was until I had a brainwave.

I was preparing for my Grade 5 Singing exam, but my singing teacher had not anticipated how quickly I would learn the repertoire for the exam. After having sung César Franck's *Panis Angelicus* ad nauseam, my teacher conceded that I could bring in some of my own repertoire and that he would gladly accompany me, as the exam was still weeks away. By chance, my mum was heading to Bond Street and asked if I needed anything from central London. Sensing my opportunity, I told her that I could sing my own stuff with my singing teacher because I was doing so well, and that if she was anywhere near Chappell of Bond Street, that the sheet music to the album she had bought for me might be in there, and I would love it if maybe she could buy it for me. But no worries if not.

With ten minutes left of my singing lesson to go, and with the exam repertoire completely covered, my teacher asked if I had brought anything along for us to play together. Wearing a broad grin, I pulled out my new but already well-thumbed sheet music book of #1's. Opening it at my favourite song from the album, *My All*, and setting it on the piano stand, I saw the look on my teacher's face sour. With an expression of disappointment, he sneered, 'It's not real music, Obi. Perhaps this was a mistake. Let's just focus on your graded exams repertoire.' As much as I loved singing Schubert, Palestrina and Mozart, the music written by European composers from centuries ago didn't feed me in the same way Motown or Whitney Houston and Mariah did. As such, impromptu performances would have to serve to sate my growing musical appetite.

One afternoon, I was singing to myself as we lined up to head back into school after lunch. On the other side of the playground, I noticed a group of boys pointing and laughing at me as they gathered around their ringleader, Paul. Paul was two years older than me, with deliberately scruffy brown hair.

'Ha! He's such a gayboy.'

I stopped, mortified. I didn't know why but the words stung. I wasn't. I didn't. I felt a burning rage inside that I was unable to express. As my skin flushed, I felt a tightening in

13

my chest and an embarrassment that muted me. I stared on as the boy, locking eyes with me, put one hand in his ear, the other stroking the air, miming a faux-diva riff while cackling to his posse. My heart became a fist. We proceeded into our respective classrooms. Sticks and stones. Words were harmless though, right?

As the week dragged on, so too did my growing sense of shame and humiliation. Our junior school being so small, there was no hiding; shared break-times and neighbouring classrooms made sure of that. I was a boy transformed. Break-times became vain attempts to camouflage myself. Every time we crossed paths, each fleeting interaction would be punctuated with a gesture and a whining vocalisation as Paul laughed to the cronies invariably flanking him. The fact that I was half a foot taller than this boy didn't matter. The power he exerted over me wasn't about just the two of us. It was about me knowing my place and making sure that I didn't step out of line – not only in the playground hierarchy but also in what was deemed acceptable for a boy to enjoy. Unfortunately for him, though, I have always had a single-minded streak, especially when it comes to my enjoyment of divas from the '90s. Waiting in the music corridor for the lesson to start after lunch, I was accosted by my diminutive tormentor and two of his friends.

'Look who it is! Gonna sing us some Whitney?'

Only the melanin in my skin stopped me from blending into the maroon of my school blazer.

'Come on, sing a song, faggot!'

In that moment, the week exploded out of me. My chest erupted, no longer a fist. The tension and bile that had been suppressed had been lanced. The blood rushed to my fingertips as they extended, my hand outstretched and swung wildly, connecting with his cheek with a firm *crack!* He staggered briefly before recovering his composure and making eye contact with me. Even in the dim corridor lighting, I could see the deep-red outline of each of my fingers imprinted along his porcelain skin. We stood for a moment, both of us with tears in our eyes, equally stunned by what had just happened and what to do now. For my part, I panicked, ashamed that I had let my temper get the better of me, hearing the voice of my parents: 'Not angry, just disappointed'. I could see my father's eyes boring deep into me as he reiterated the importance of a 'thick skin'. This boy had two witnesses who had seen it all and would be able to corroborate exactly what had happened. And yet, as the remainder of our respective classes approached, he wiped his tears away and led his classmates to stand at the door of his form room. We never spoke about that moment. Nor did he ever say another word to me.

I for one was embarrassed. Angry, certainly, but it lasted mere moments before it gave way to an overwhelming sense of shame. I knew that what we had both done was wrong. I think he did too. In that moment, yoked by the violence we had both enacted on one another, all we could do was cry. I think I expected that there might be some sense of catharsis, some vindication for my actions that would acquit me of the charge those older boys levied at me: the charge of being a 'faggot'. At the age of nine, the insults that flowed most consistently from the mouths of my classmates were variants of homophobic slurs. Despite many of us not knowing for certain what our sexual preference was, or even what sex was for that matter, the one thing we knew for sure was that it was the gravest of insults. The violence of this experience demonstrated clearly why I felt so resistant to the mantra of 'sticks and stones' that was fed to me as a child. It ignored something that children inherently know and intuit: language has power. In the wrong hands, this power means that language can cause damage and lead to discomfort that is often longer lasting than physical violence.

When a bone is broken in the body, if it is reset properly it will heal to be just as strong as it was before. But the incorrect alignment of the bone for healing can cause it to become twisted, bent and swollen – a malunion. Words may not cause physical injury, but they can mould, crack and fracture your self-identity. The violence that played out between my harasser and me in that corridor was borne of a need to use our respective 'rods of correction'. I cannot speak for why he felt compelled to keep me in line nor do I know if the tears that welled in his eyes were the result of recognising the pain we had caused each other. I can say that the shame I felt was two-fold: firstly, that I had lashed out so violently, but also that the F-word that precipitated my action fractured and threatened my self-identity so much in that moment. While today I identify as a straight, cisgender man, I look back on all of us as pre-teens at that school with a deep sense of pity, regardless of how we now identify, for the way in which we had our self-identity broken and misshapen; saddened by the constant barrage of narratives and correction that led to the malunions in the men that we would become.

Narratives and storytelling are fundamental to what it is to be human. The French film director Jean-Luc Godard, whose films *Masculin Féminin* and *Two or Three Things I Know About Her* I would later watch over and over, once said, 'Sometimes reality is too complex. Stories give it form.' I learned about the form of the world I was growing up in through the stories I was surrounded by and fed. Sometimes I was aware of the life lessons I was being taught, and at other times it was more subconscious. I grew up in a faith that had solely men leading the services. When parents collected their children from the school gates, it was almost always mothers who did the school run. If I watched a Disney film, the hero was invariably a male character with his prize being societal acclaim and, more often than not, a bride. Unbeknown to me, I was being taught what a 'romantic hero' looked like. But not just me. We all were.

Discussing what costumes we would wear for an upcoming Disney-themed party, as we waited at the school gates one day to be collected by our parents, I listened as the tween-to-be whose birthday party it was, assembled his dream cast. 'You could be Gaston ... you have to be John Smith ...' Arriving at me, he was stumped for a moment but then pressed on. 'Ooh, you could be something from *The Lion King*. Like Mufasa or Simba.' There was no intended malice, nor did I internalise it as such. This was just the form of the world. If I *was* to be an animated beau, being of African descent, it was less of a stretch for me to undergo a leonine transformation than to be blonde or blue-eyed. The author Rudine Sims Bishop said of storytelling:

> Books are sometimes windows, offering views of worlds that may be real or imagined, familiar or strange. These windows are also sliding glass doors, and readers have only to walk through in imagination to become part of whatever world has been created or recreated by the author. When lighting conditions are just right, however, a window can also be a mirror. Literature transforms human experience and reflects it back to us, and in that reflection we can see our own lives and experiences as part of a larger human experience. Reading, then, becomes a means of self-affirmation, and readers often seek their mirrors in books.

As I grew up, I would come to realise that although I relished peering through windows, I would never quite catch my reflection. Rather, I would be presented with a funhouse mirror that created a visage I recognised, but that jarred me. Devouring stories as I did, the constant compromise of peering into worlds in which I never truly saw myself would leave me perennially peckish.

My insatiable appetite for stories begins with my father. Whether he was reading *Watership Down* at bedtime to me and my brothers or playing audiobooks as we undertook the long car journey across the country to get the ferry to Ireland on family holidays, he recognised the power a story has as a communal experience. One of the films that would frequently make an appearance on our regular Friday film nights, with the whole family cuddled up on the sofa, was the story of the boxing underdog, *Rocky*. Never shy of using everything as a teachable moment, my father would give his running commentary extolling the virtues of both Rocky Balboa and the reigning champ Apollo Creed as we passed around homemade popcorn.

'You see? It's about never giving up! Anything is possible if you just keep going.' Growing up in a house that had a poster of Muhammad Ali on the back of the bathroom door, I was always bemused that the hero of this story was played by Sylvester Stallone, as I had never known a white champion heavyweight boxer. But as the horns of the soundtrack willed Rocky on through his training, montaging his way through punching meat, jump push-ups, and culminating in his run up the steps to the entrance of the Philadelphia Museum of Art, an idol was cemented in boyhood.

While I didn't fancy myself as a boxer, for me Rocky transcended sport or race. This was just what an ideal man was:

brave, hardworking and dedicated. In much the same way as the many animated films I watched, his prize was societal acclaim and, by the story's end, the love of a woman, Adrian Pennino. I thought nothing of the fact that when Adrian is in Rocky's apartment and says she doesn't know him well enough, feels uncomfortable and would like to leave, he corners her with his hand on the door, barring her exit. As an alpha male, our protagonist, who by the end of the film we are rooting for, must sometimes be assertive in love as well as in the ring. The message of that scene to audiences was that a woman is not to be trusted with her own volition. Even though she was visibly uncomfortable and felt like she wanted to extricate herself from that situation, the agency that she had in the situation was ripe to be trampled on by our protagonist, who knew her mind better than she knew it herself. As a strong man, he could protect her from her abusive brother; he was her knight in shining armour – she just couldn't see it at first. But sometimes, not even the most 'heroic' knight has gentlemanly intentions.

When I first watched the film *Sixteen Candles*, it was on the same well-used sofas with my brothers and parents. The Molly Ringwald teen classic about 16-year-old Sam coming of age and crushing on Jake, the 18-year-old heartthrob of the school, was, according to my older brother, essential viewing. Watching Ringwald's character fall for Jake Ryan, I saw his older girlfriend Caroline as an obstacle to the narrative arc of the story. It seemed to me to be narratively justified when, during a party at his house, Jake is repulsed by Caroline's drunkenness and subsequently dismisses her to the freshman, Ted, saying that he can 'get a piece of ass anytime'. Her sexual availability is almost evidence that Jake has outgrown her. Later, when Jake offers Ted the opportunity to drive Caroline home, he reassures Ted that she's 'so blitzed' she won't know the difference between the two boys. It is played for laughs, her semi-conscious body carried and manoeuvred into the passenger seat of Jake's car. That there is an implied date-rape is glossed over when the following morning, waking up in the car, Ted asks if she enjoyed it, to which she replies, 'You know, I have this weird feeling I did.' That she had her consent violated was just par for the course for these two boys, and any moral wrongdoing countered by the fact that Caroline 'enjoyed' it. From Disney princes to heavyweight boxers to high school heartthrobs, winning over the opposite sex – and success with them – was seen as one of the markers of being a successful man.

Growing up in the '90s in the UK, it would be remiss of me to try to lay the blame for the sexualisation or objectification of women solely at the feet of Hollywood. But whereas blockbuster films had the British Board of Film Classification doling out '15' or '18' ratings for films with too much violence or sexual content – and since 1964 British broadcasters have adhered to a watershed, prohibiting the broadcasting of certain adult content before 9pm – print media was a different story.

On 17 November 1970, in an attempt to compete with

the *Daily Mirror*, which was regularly publishing photos of women in lingerie and bikinis, Stephanie Rahn appeared on Page 3 of *The Sun* wearing, as the newspaper's editor Larry Lamb would describe later in an attempt to explain the decision, her 'birthday suit'. The newspaper would go on to print photos of topless women on its third page for the next 44 years, changing the face of British print media forever. Its advocates would argue that it granted women opportunities and empowered them, with several going on to pursue successful careers as models, singers and presenters. Its critics would argue that it was sexist and demeaning to women, with the use of topless models as young as 16 attracting particular ire, until a law change in 2003.

One of the most strident opponents was Labour MP Clare Short, who in 1986 introduced a Private Members' Bill proposing the banning of Page 3 topless models, later commenting that it 'degrades women and our country'. *The Sun* would reply by branding Short a 'killjoy'. It quoted three Page 3 girls, who described her as 'jealous' and 'fat and ugly', asking in its leader column, 'who are we to disagree with their verdict?'

Whatever opposition there may have been to this editorial decision in the public sphere died down long before I was born. My parents chose a more personal form of resistance by allowing only *The Guardian*, *The Independent* and occasionally the *Daily Mirror* ('your granny is fond of the *Mirror*') on the dining room table. There was a tacit understanding that *The Sun* was not to be brought into the house.

Unfortunately, children have foolish hearts. Having stolen glimpses of Page 3 across the shoulders of commuters on my way to school, my curiosity began to get the better of me. This was only exacerbated by a fellow Year 7 boy showing off his copy early one morning, a crowd of his peers clambering over him, desperate to get a glimpse of the bare breasts. In an attempt to quell the noise the growing early-morning rabble was causing, lest we attract the attention of a teacher, he said simply, 'Guys, just buy one from the newsagents. They can't stop you from buying it. It's a newspaper, not porn!'

He was of course correct. At our all-boys Catholic school, sex education was somewhat lacking in nuance. Perhaps the titters from a room full of pubescent boys meant our biology teachers only engaged with the topic superficially. Or maybe it was the dated sex-ed VHS that left us uninterested and uninformed. Taking matters into our own hands, aware there was no legal bar to our buying the paper, and hungry for further research materials, many of us learned what we could about the opposite sex from tabloid newspapers that considered naked sixteen-year-olds to be acceptable accompaniments to the weather forecast and other breaking news.

Where film and televised media agreed that there should be some protection afforded to children from content more suited to an adult audience, certain elements of the British print media resisted the notion for over four decades. So when, aged eleven, I approached the counter of my local newsagent in my school uniform with a copy of the red-top in my hand, armed with 30p and nerves fortified by peer pressure, all my local shopkeeper could do was give me a quizzical look. Sensing his apprehension, I erupted, blurting out the superfluous exposition of a kid worried that the scent of the guilt he's feeling cannot be masked by any amount of Lynx body spray. 'Oh yeah ... that, that's for my uncle who's staying with us but he is over from Ireland. He's ... he loves ... he just asked if I could pick it up for him because he's tired and had long flight.'

He looked back at me, almost imperceptibly shaking his head in what I took to be disapproval, and accepted the coins proffered by my outstretched hand. Desperate to play it cool, I stole home, paper in hand, trying not to sprint. Finally at my door, just as I was turning the key, I heard my mother's voice behind me asking for help bringing in the shopping from the car. How had I not seen her?

'Sure, Mum,' I mumbled, as I dropped my schoolbag by the front door. My hard-earned prize, however, I was less willing to let out of my sight. I stuffed it under my blazer while shuttling Safeway bags stuffed with groceries from the car to the house. Tasked with locking the car on my final run, I was on the precipice of success when, as I crossed the threshold to my house, the tabloid slipped from my armpit just as my mother joined me to see if I needed a hand. The guilt I'd sensed in the newsagent's morphed into shame, as my mother and I locked onto the foreign object. My mother waited for her usually verbose son to meet her gaze, but I couldn't. Wracking my brain for some plausible alternative reason why I'd bought the paper, which might extricate me from the mortifying discomfiture I was in, I landed on, 'There's a thing, the section on Arsenal ... there's some sport ... ' I gave up. It was pointless.

Looking back, as the mother of three boys and scores of foster children, I'm certain it wasn't the first time she'd had to deal with a similarly awkward situation. But in that moment, my silent prayer for a seismic event to disappear me through the doorway of our Holloway Road house reached nearly pietistic levels. As she picked up the now crumpled newspaper, she gave me a kindly look of part disappointment, part pity. 'Obi, these pictures aren't for children. There's no need to rush to grow up. You'll get there soon enough.'

Though my parents tried valiantly to shield me from adult images, the narratives that surrounded me about what it meant to be a man or woman, white or Black, gay or straight were all pervasive. Over the course of the forty-plus years that Page 3 ran, and the hundreds of models who graced their pages, only four Black women were featured. In Britain, it seemed – from advertising to the softcore pornography of the tabloids – beauty had a specific look. Women were there to be objectified and leered over, won as prizes and as extensions of men of all ages. If you were foolish enough to show too close an association with them, admiring their talent or seeing them as role models, you were a deemed by your peers to be an outcast to the point of treachery. The ultimate betrayal was to be homosexual, and even if the adults around you never said it, your mates would be quick enough to make you aware of it. While I had already felt the stinging violence of those words from school, they pierced a lot deeper when they came from those in my own home.

Being of mixed heritage, my Nigerian father and Irish mother were always very conscious of trying to ensure that we engaged with our cultural heritage, whether it was the jollof rice we would eat with my Nigerian grandparents and cousins or the after-school Irish music classes we would attend at the local Irish community centre. After playing the tin whistle at a local ceilidh and watching the phenomenal Irish dancers, I told my mum I'd love to try it. Mum and Dad, always far too obliging, signed me up and tolerated six months of my prancing around in the living room. Making steady enough progress, I was so excited when my dance teacher told me that I would need to buy some jig shoes as I was moving up a class. I would unfortunately never wear them.

The following week, as my mum waited in the car, she sent in my older brother to come and collect me from the class. I grinned, catching his eye through the door, as this was his first time watching me dance as part of a cohort rather than interrupting his viewing of *The Simpsons*. Heading to join my mum, he observed, 'Ha! You're the only boy in the class. Why'd you like it so much? Is it 'cos you're gay?' I remember crying off sick the next class. Then

I feigned losing interest to my mum. Finally I asked her to return the shoes. It wasn't for me and it was just a waste of everyone's time and money.

I don't blame my brother for that comment. It was offhand and trivial in his mind. The same boy who had mocked my fan-boying over Mariah was in his form at school; homophobic slurs were *de rigueur* in both his class and my own. But hearing it from my own flesh and blood was a rod of correction that caught me unawares, the violence of it unsuspected, coming from a boy I admired so deeply, who I wanted to match in height, wit and confidence. Rebutting lessons from those I didn't like or felt no affinity to felt simple enough. But withstanding such criticism is much tougher when it comes from those who genuinely care about you; it demands more compromise. As I scrabbled around trying to decipher the form of the world, I tried to be more discerning of the lessons I learned, and from whom I was learning them. However, decoding what it was to be a young Black man was not always straightforward.

Piling in the school showers after games can be daunting for many schoolboys, but my friend Mark and I insisted on washing our entire bodies rather than opting for the notional flirtation with the water that was the preferred shower routine of the majority of my classmates, so we always rushed to be first. Of Jamaican heritage, Mark was one of my closest friends both on and off the rugby pitch. Bantering about some first-year gossip or other, we had the showers to ourselves momentarily one day when we heard one of our white classmates shout loud enough for the whole changing room to hear: 'Nah, don't go in there with Mark and Obi ... they'll knock you out with those things,' to which the whole room erupted into fits of laughter.

Mark and I exchanged uneasy glances, aware that anything too lingering might be misconstrued. They were talking about our genitals. Our pubescent penises would become the butt of years-long running jokes about their size from friends and teammates who thought it both hilarious and rooted in truth. To this day, none of my male friends have seen my erect penis, and I'd wager they haven't seen Mark's either. But that wouldn't get in the way of the joke, which was that Black penises were hilariously oversized. Even before the advent of high-speed broadband and the smorgasbord of niche porn categories to which users nowadays have access, my twelve-year-old peers had already internalised the idea that Black men were more sexual than white men. Having learned this lesson they would teach it to others.

The uneasy glance that Mark and I shared seemed to speak volumes. Do we shut this down? Do we accept it? It's a compliment, right? Did we believe it to be true? Our tacit acceptance of the joke seemed like the only logical thing to do. It had to be true, right? It didn't need to be said; we both knew that what differentiated us from the rest of the class was our African heritage. Once again, media of all description would praise men who were well endowed and mock those whose penises were too small. Having not seen another man's erection, my points of comparison were very limited, so I was relying on the stories told to me by those who apparently *did* know what a 'normal penis' looked like – one of my white classmates, who asserted it so boldly I believed him. The whole class did. Perhaps this was just like the drumming in the music class; that to my white contemporaries the fact that I had a Black father gifted me an advantage. What was it about our life education that created such an unexamined racial divide between white and Black boys?

'I love sex, I love it. I can't do shit no more. And I'm blessed. I'm big bone-ded. I'm heavy structured. I'm hung low. If I pull my shit out this whole room get dark.'

Watching the talented Bernie Mac brag to a full auditorium about his penis size during one of his first appearances on *Def Comedy Jam*, I was taken by his confidence and bravado. The stand-up comedy show helped launch the careers of dozens of African-American comics as they performed to largely Black audiences. Bernie lodged himself into my memory in the way things often do with teenagers, with only half a sentence needed before my brother and I would do our best Mac impressions in unison, cackling to each other as we mimicked him. It wasn't just in our household that Bernie would be referenced. In his collaboration with Christina Aguilera on the 2002 No.1 hit *Dirrty*, the rapper Redman would invoke the skit, boasting that he was '*blessed, and hung low*, like Bernie Mac'.

Many men not only equate penis size with masculinity and sexual competence, but also believe the average penis to be bigger than it is in reality, leading to an unfortunate disconnect. In one recent study by the University of Sheffield, 45 per cent of men responded that they would like a larger penis, while 85 per cent of women respondents reported being very happy with their partner's penis size. What research there is on the matter, taking into account the bias of self-reporting, indicates there being an average standard deviation of roughly an inch globally with regard to ethnicity. Whatever the truth of the matter, I was in an education system that was intent on believing certain stories about young Black boys. I did not feel deeply inclined to start evangelising to my peers or potential dates about the truth behind these stories about my perceived attributes, be they physical or sexual. Watching these Black men wear their confidence and pride unapologetically, I was aware enough that their swagger was performative; that their self-confidence felt like an armoured reclamation of a narrative they hadn't been in control of as they spoke to an audience of people who looked like them. It felt like a safe harbour; an oasis against the daily niggles and injustices I would face at school.

Teaching at any state school is a truly monumental task, with many teachers often going above and beyond the job description to ensure their students receive the best education. The unenviable task of teaching at an all-boys school feels like a special kind of purgatory. From my perspective, the disruption caused by idle chatter or students distracting each other didn't seem to follow any particular racial pattern. None of my teachers, I'm sure, would openly admit to having more of a problem with Black students than their white counterparts. They would fear being called a racist. And yet, the national statistics tell a different story, with Black African, Black Caribbean and Mixed-race boys having some of the highest rates of exclusion in the country, at least double that of their white counterparts.

Mark and I would witness first-hand the unfortunate phenomenon of 'Racism without Racists', as observed by Eduardo Bonilla-Silva in his book of the same name. During the entirety of my eleven years at the school, there were only five Black members of the teaching staff. In retrospect, I cannot help but think that had there been more Black teachers at the all-boys' school, the following disruptions that Black students suffered might have been avoided and literally hundreds of Black students' education not been unnecessarily impacted.

Hair must be of a straightforward style, tidy and clear of the face and shirt collar, and must retain its natural colour. The face must be clean-shaven and sideboards must not extend below the middle of the ear. Peculiar, ostentatious or bizarre styles are unacceptable. Examples of unacceptable styles are: bleached, dyed, tinted or highlighted hair; closely cropped hair (including cuts described as 'numbers 1, 2 or 3').

That was the wording given in the school rulebook. The reasoning for the rule was never given, but the unintended consequences were undeniable. Barred from 'ostentatious' hairstyles like corn rows or twists, one of the few options Black men have in schools or formal workplaces is to keep their hair cut neat and short. While I was aware that Black barbershops existed, and were a source of pride for many of my Black friends to receive their 'shape-ups', me and my siblings' hair grew at a prodigious rate. My father could not find it in himself to justify paying for three boys to make monthly trips to the barbers. So, for the next two decades, the Ugoala boys had their locks cut by Eze Ugoala. Every month or so, armed with hair trimmers purchased more than ten years previously, he would dress each of us in a barber's gown and, in the mirror-strewn bathroom, cut back the latest growth of tight Afro coils.

Having had at least one of his sons in the school for six years by this point, my father had always very carefully abided by the rules of the school, keeping our hair an appropriate length, while bemoaning the fact that he could not go shorter. Afro hair has a very awkward in-between stage between grades 2–3 and full Afro that is neither capable of being styled nor short enough to be ordered. Approaching twelve years of age, I was beginning to explore my hair, letting my 4B curls grow out. I loved it – its reaction to water. I took particular joy in my ability to look like a 'Jackson cousin' if I blow-dried it out. It grew to be a source of pride. But it also drew mockery and teasing.

Sitting in the second row of my music class one day, I could hear tittering behind me. But no matter how often I turned around the boys behind me gave nothing away, leaving me with the unnerving sense that I was the butt of a joke that everybody was in on but me. It was only towards the end of the lesson that I ran my hands through the back of my hair and felt two IKEA pencils fall out of my curls and onto the floor. The boys in the row behind me roared with laughter. I brushed it off and laughed along, claiming the pencils. 'Ha! These are mine now!' Returning home, I dropped my bag by the front door, barely greeting my parents as I climbed the stairs to the bathroom and plugged in the clippers in front of the mirror, setting about butchering the curls at the back of my skull. In my impulsivity, that was all that mattered. My hair had betrayed me; the source of my pride was now the source of hilarity to my classmates. I'm not sure exactly what my parents must have thought when I arrived downstairs for dinner that evening with my impromptu self-styled high-top, but they didn't prod too far. Dad wouldn't comment on it other than after dinner, when he suggested that I went up to the bathroom and he would tidy up my rather rushed attempt at self-grooming.

Perhaps it was the drastic change to my hair length – even though my dad had been cutting the Ugoala boys' hair to the school's regulations for years by this point – but the following day, after assembly, the deputy headmaster informed me that I must report to reception. 'Your hair is too short, so you're going to have to spend the next few days in isolation.' I briefly protested that, like always, it was a regulation '4' haircut, but my pleas were in vain. The seemingly arbitrary decision to dole out this punishment, despite my certainty that my father hadn't erred, led to a growing sense of mistrust in those charged with my education. That I would spend the next two days out of lessons and away from my teachers felt discordant in words that I didn't have the language to express.

Although that was my first and only time in exclusion for 'hair violations', I would often note the absence of classmates as the register was read out and, after a momentary pause, a classmate would inform the teacher, 'Oh yeah, exclusion. Hair.' Walking past the exclusion room over the years, I noticed the pupils were almost exclusively of Black heritage. Perhaps if there had been a more diverse teaching staff they might have noted that for many Black boys raised by Black fathers, society had told them that a 'professional hairstyle' meant a 'short, back and sides'. They might even have queried what value extricating Black students from a classroom would bring to a year group. Unfortunately, during my time there, that question was never asked.

The rules, my teachers would often say, were not written by them. But it was their job to enforce them. I felt unnerved by the subjective application of the 'peculiar, ostentatious or bizarre' hair rule that was so often brought to bear upon Black students by certain, invariably white, teachers who were 'just enforcing the rules'. Upon entering a classroom where students were talking, it was not a rarity for the teacher to single out, among a sea of white faces, the few Black faces for making an unacceptable amount of noise. When challenged as to why they were being pinpointed in this dubious discernment when the rabble was class wide, the familiar refrain came back of 'I don't care if everybody was talking, yours was just the first face I saw.' When the inevitable after-school detention came, despite the obvious inability for one student to summon a chorus of voices thirty-fold to be heard outside a classroom, the detention hall seemed to be disproportionately filled with Black boys.

One particular after-school detainment was awarded due to lunchtime shenaniganising in the playground. Being in Zone 2 in London, space was limited. As such, a further draconian law was put in place that prohibited running around in the playground – to stop general boisterousness and younger boys from being knocked into. As the song tells us, young hearts do run free and, as autumn approached, the joy that the eleven- to fourteen-year-olds elicited in trying to catch falling leaves from the oversized oak tree in the centre of the playground would be the highlight of an otherwise restrictive day. That was until the deputy head-master caught wind of this particular lunchtime diversion. The same teacher who had chastised me for the length of my hair descended on the playground with the stealth of a jungle cat and, his prey once caught, issued the burden of reporting to him for after-school detention. I have no shame in saying I took part in said game that afternoon, and only a little in admitting that every leaf eluded me. I could not, however, elude the deputy headmaster. As I arrived for the detention, the familiar sight of a sea of Black students corralled for punishment caught my attention. But that was the form of the world. Black boys just get in trouble more often.

'Sir?'

The room looked up from their detention assignment to a Ghanaian boy in the year above me who had his hand raised.

'Sir!' he insisted, this time more forcefully.

'Yes, Michael, what is it?'

'Sir, don't you think it's a bit weird that even though all of first, second AND third form were playing that game that the only students who are in detention are Black?'

His tone was so genuinely querying that it was disarming, like a maths student struggling with an equation. The implication however was not one that would be taken with an iota of the benefit of the doubt.

'How DARE you?' roared the deputy headmaster, suddenly crimson with cheeks ruddied, as he rose from his desk and strode towards Michael. 'I would never in my life . . . how dare . . . right! Everybody else, go home. Michael, report to my office.'

I never followed up with Michael. There wasn't anything much else to say. I heard he was issued with a two-hour detention on a Saturday. Our custodians, as much as they cared about us and undertook the Herculean task of being educators, would often fail at creating an educational landscape of parity. Whether that was within the structure of the school or examining their own biases within the classroom, Black boys scrabbling to find their place in the world were constantly crudely reminded that double standards would be at play. If teachers and educators, storytellers and writers, editors and journalists did nothing to examine or modify their own behaviour, then young men and women would grow up with grossly damaging ideas about race and gender. As glad as my parents were that they had sent me to a Catholic state school with a great music programme, my faith, my passion for music and my self-identity as a young Black man would come to be misshapen, broken and fractured over the following decade at the school by the very people charged with my care.

2

Shackles

By the time I was sixteen our school choir had garnered quite the reputation as one of the leading boys' choirs in the country. When we were invited to perform at the Live Earth concert at the Cathedral of Rome, the Basilica of St John Lateran, it was both a privilege and a chance for me to go on an international holiday with some of my closest choir friends. Those of us in the sixth form had privileges, one of which meant we could stay up playing cards in the hotel courtyard while the music staff enjoyed a glass of Italian wine in the evening air. The serenity of the still-warm dusk came to a jolting halt when the school chaplain came over and said, very plainly, 'Now, Obi, remember, you must go to bed five minutes before everybody else. We need extra time to secure your shackles. Can't have you running off into the night now, can we?'

As the only Black choral scholar, the meaning was clear, the invocation obvious. The choice of language was blatant.

My reaction however, as it has had to be throughout my life, was tempered. The rage I felt was delayed by the sheer nonchalance and audacity of the statement. Even though I could feel it building, the bluntness of the assertion caged me in rigidity. I looked to my best friend in the choir. He said nothing. Not long afterwards, everybody went to bed – at the same time.

My friend and I were sharing a room on this trip. He had heard the barbed edict, but stayed mute. Dr King once said, 'We will remember not the words of our enemies, but the silence of our friends.' But I remember it all, vividly – from the size of the pebbles on the floor of the piazza to the fellow staff members who, sensing I had been crushed by the weight of those cruel words, tittered awkwardly in response. In that deathly quiet Italian dorm room, once I was certain my friend was asleep, I cried myself to sleep, furious at my impotence, at his cowardice, but mainly at the language of this 'man of God'. *Shackles*.

I was twelve years old when, during the summer holidays, I first watched the ABC miniseries *Roots*. I was aware of the transatlantic slave trade as a child but, as my father is Igbo Nigerian, felt somehow disconnected from the trauma of the collective atrocity which saw an estimated 12.5 million Africans seized, sold and shipped to the so-called 'New World', disembarking in the Caribbean and North and South America. My father, however, deemed it essential viewing for us all, and I watched in horror as the actor I knew as *Star Trek*'s Geordie La Forge was shackled and captured. Watching the scene where he is seized, I felt a visceral reaction as he struggles to the point of exhaustion to escape his manacles. His eventual acceptance of his captivity, the breaking of his will as he realises that the metal chains that bind him will not shift or break, resonated in my heart in a way that, as a child, I couldn't verbalise. Watched by his captors, he acknowledges his own impotency.

Conversations would happen over dinner. My parents would listen patiently as I tried, alongside my brothers, to wrestle with it all. It was during one of these evening conversations, which would extend long past the table being cleared of any morsel of food, that my parents reiterated a point they had made many times before: that growing up in London, life would always be different for us boys as young Black men.

'But Dad, I'm as much Irish as I am Nigerian.'

'I know that, son. But in this country that doesn't matter. Just ask your older brothers. That's not how you will be seen.'

My heart sank as I saw the tacit confirmation in the eyes of my eldest brother, Chijioke. I turned to Alaeze, whose shrug confirmed my father's worldview, and wrapped my childlike naïveté in a dolorous cloak. These three men were my idols, my first touchstones as to how to be in the world. For my father, his awareness that he was raising children in a society that would often flatten the complexity of our identities did nothing to dampen his optimism about who we could be or what we could go on to achieve. I don't believe that my father is alone in believing that every child should be given the best opportunities in life, with no door closed in their face. How heartbreaking it must then be for a parent to witness their child mature as the world around them, from friends to teachers to the wider media, actively attempts to close doors in their face. Noting my lingering discomfort as bedtime approached, my dad hugged me and said, 'Obi, the world doesn't get to decide who you are. That is on you. If you work hard enough and put in the effort, *you* get to decide your place in the world; nobody else. You can be whatever you want to be.'

The maelstrom of emotions evoked by watching *Roots* instilled in me an unexpected courage. Returning after that summer to my second year in the senior school, I was sat at the back of the music classroom one day when my teacher from the previous year waltzed in. After some idle small talk with his colleague, he demanded my attention. Beating on the top of the grand piano, they waited expectantly with the air of a comic delivering a 'knock knock' joke.

I paused.

I seethed.

The class waited for my response to the charade they had seen time and time again in this classroom. This time, it would be different.

'Sir, don't do that please. It's racist.'

Basilisk-esque, I saw the colour drain from his face as we locked eyes. The air disappeared from the room as near silence descended, broken only by the oscillating glances of my classmates darting back and forth between the teacher and me, caught in a deadlock of who would speak next.

'Yes, Obi. Of course.'

He promptly left the room and the 'drumming joke' was never referenced or mentioned again. Something was lost, but ultimately something was gained. Did I miss being special? Different? Unique in my Blackness? Of course. And yet I still carry the shame attached to my complicity in that class humiliation for indulging the joke the first time, and on each subsequent occasion.

For the best part of a year, I had permitted my classmates and my teachers to use my heritage as the butt of a joke that I had not initiated. I would love to say that I didn't know it was wrong, but it is only recently, decades later, that I have seen fit to discuss the incident with my parents. My parents had sought out a phenomenal school for me that in many ways opened up the doors they feared would have been closed in my face. Would they have long tolerated my presence in a school where the music teachers tapped out 'African' rhythms on the table as a faux form of communication? Or where the priest charged with the spiritual wellbeing of the students felt comfortable mocking them with jokes about slavery? I did not dare find out. The world was not built for me, or for people who looked like me. All that was left for me to do was to try not to compromise myself too much, swallow the necessary bitter pills that were part of the journey and work hard enough to be the person I had the potential to become. And yet, for all the shame that I internalised as a child, as a disillusioned adult who has himself worked as an educator, I feel a certain level of revulsion towards a teacher and a priest who chose to consciously other one of the only Black students in their care.

The dehumanising of Black people is a narrative that has been told for centuries. I remind myself when thinking too critically of my schoolboy self that I should not have had to swallow bitter pills and that my teachers and school chaplain failed me in those moments. I placate myself with the knowledge that my small act of resistance in that classroom, finally unyoking myself from that racist narrative, might just have protected another Black student in the school from being the punch line to a racist joke.

On why he felt compelled to become a writer, the Pulitzer-prize winning author Junot Díaz explained:

You guys know about vampires? ... You know, vampires have no reflections in a mirror? There's this idea that monsters don't have reflections in a mirror. And what I've always thought isn't that monsters don't have reflections in a mirror. It's that if you want to make a human being into a monster, deny them, at the cultural level, any reflection of themselves.

While he would go on to echo Rudine Sims Bishop's windows/mirror analogy about representation in literature, Díaz also captured a larger truth about how society has set itself up. The creation of 'monsters' is a necessity for a society that seeks to justify why those who would otherwise be deemed as human may be treated inhumanely. The depictions of Jewish people in the thirteenth century as 'Aaron, Son of the Devil', the nineteenth-century depiction of all non-Europeans as 'savages', and the modern habit of designating men killed in drone strikes on foreign territory as 'unlawful combatants' (unless explicit intelligence posthumously proves them innocent) share origins and serve the same purpose: creating an outsider or monster that a society can direct its ire towards.

The suppression of instinctive human empathy is most effective when it is attached to a good narrative. Xenophobia in the UK is a story that dates back centuries. Be it the enforcement of the papal bull of 1218, which decreed Jewish people must wear clothing to distinguish themselves, or the 3.1 million enslaved Africans who were bought and transported as Britain played its role in the transatlantic slave triangle, the fearmongering around those who aren't 'native' to the British Isles has long been the justification for 'strong borders' and foreign intervention. Just as the romantic hero of narrative cinema assumes that his role of protector will be rewarded with marriage, it was a man's job – his duty even – to ensure the protection of the innocent and defenceless women of Britain.

This story shall the good man teach his son;
And Crispin Crispian shall ne'er go by,
From this day to the ending of the world,
But we in it shall be remember'd;
We few, we happy few, we band of brothers;
For he to-day that sheds his blood with me
Shall be my brother; be he ne'er so vile,
This day shall gentle his condition:
And gentlemen in England now a-bed
Shall think themselves accursed they were not here,
And hold their manhoods cheap whiles any speaks
That fought with us upon Saint Crispin's day.

From *Henry V*, Act IV, Scene III

From schoolboy age through to my conservatoire training as an actor, the prominence given to certain stories and certain playwrights was perhaps no better encapsulated than the consistent reappearance of William Shakespeare. When I won a place to train at the Drama Centre London, I was told that we were being given a 'Classical Actor's Education' within which 'The Bard' would feature heavily. This was the reason given for why we had twice the number of men in our cohort as women; 'it's just representative of the industry' was the justification I remember one tutor giving (perhaps all the more galling when I later learned that twice the number of young women auditioned for a place than their male counterparts). The preference for male-centric stories, even those that were hundreds of years old, would affect my fellow actors in training and still has ripple effects in the industry today as theatres not only decide who will be on their stages, but also what stories around war and gender they will give prominence, as I would soon learn.

As I toured from China and then to New York listening to Alex Hassell rouse his troops in the Royal Shakespeare Company tour of *Henry V*, I began to feel a sense of unease at how moved I was by the performance. Between Hassell's undoubted skill as an actor and Shakespeare's language, I would leave the scene, on the eve of battle, pumped as if I were *actually* going to war. To believe Henry, this would be the making of a man – to go to war for your monarch and your country. I would regale my children of our glorious victory, and those who did not fight alongside me would be lesser men. I felt primed for an imaginary battle in the safety of the Brooklyn Academy of Music with my manly pride suitably stoked and encouraged. As I looked round at the other men (as the cast was largely comprised of men) on stage, I wondered, was this 'masculine energy' inbuilt? Was it nature or nurture?

I had always felt at home playing with toy guns or fighting video games. I was accustomed to warding off the charge of being a 'wuss' or a 'little bitch' on the rugby field by shrugging off injury and pain and 'soldiering on' regardless. I learned not to express my emotions, except in private, lest I be stuck with the moniker of a 'sissy'. Was this a shared experience of my fellow actors on stage? That men have throughout the history of British armies had to be bribed, coerced, shamed, enlisted and tricked into battle flies in the face of the received notion that they instinctively long for battle or ache to charge into battle crying, 'For Harry, England and Saint George', as Shakespeare might have us believe.

Across the Atlantic, Samuel Lyman Atwood Marshall had a team of historians working for him who conducted individual and mass interviews with thousands of soldiers in more than four hundred infantry companies immediately after they had been in contact with enemy troops in the Second World War. The results were consistent: only 15–20 per cent of US soldiers would fire at the enemy. Author Dave Grossman, who wrote the book *On Killing* based on Marshall's findings, would write, 'the simple and demonstrable fact that there is within most men an intense resistance to killing their fellow man. A resistance so strong that, in many circumstances, soldiers on the battlefield will die before they can overcome it.'

It seemed I was not alone in my not being genetically predestined to be bloodthirsty or violent. Why, then, was my fighting spirit awoken onstage? According to Tom Digby, author of *Love and War: How Militarism Shapes Sexuality and Romance*, 'Men are culturally programmed to take on the warrior role, regardless of whether they ever go to war or not.' So from action figures and video games, to contact sport and body image, Digby argues that masculinity as a social construct in many patriarchal cultures is tied to violence and being a suitable warrior.

The fear of the threat of foreign men to British women served as another useful tool to shame men to enlist, lest they 'hold their manhoods cheap'; the feathers pinned by a group of English women called the 'White Feather Brigade' to the lapels of men who abdicated their 'masculine duties' of going to war to protect them heaped shame upon men who had not yet enlisted. However, when the British government called upon the men of Commonwealth countries to help defend 'the Motherland' in the midst of the Great War, and British women demanded their own enfranchisement after taking up wartime employment, the dual narratives of the danger posed by the lascivious, foreign invading men and the helpless woman who must be taken care of became harder to uphold. The warrior role they had been, as Digby puts it, 'culturally programmed' to assume was under dual threat: they were neither the 'man of the house' nor 'defenders of the realm' from foreign, so-called invaders.

Unfortunately, the effects of centuries of dehumanising narratives are not easily undone. The perceived threat of the monsters Díaz spoke about ignited racial tensions across the country in 1919, as almost three million soldiers returned home to a post-war Britain to compete for jobs and the attentions of British women with new arrivals from West Africa and the Caribbean. In port cities that were already ethnically diverse, the cities became powder kegs. From Glasgow to Hull, and Salford to Cardiff and London, the tension was widespread and violent, with some of the worst of the violence occurring in Liverpool.

On 5 June 1919, a young Bermudan by the name of Charles Wotton, who had served in the Royal Navy during the Great War, was chased through the streets of Liverpool to the Queen's Dock, part of the Port of Liverpool. Accounts differ as to whether he was thrown or pushed into the water, but what is known is that Wotton was struck by a rock to the head in the River Mersey and subsequently died. In the unrest that followed, groups of hundreds, sometimes thousands were reported to walk the streets attacking Black-occupied homes and hostels as Black men fled to police stations for their own protection.

The secretary of the local community centre, the Ethiopian Hall, Mr D. T. Aleifasakure Toummanah pleaded the case of some 70 men who had taken refuge against attack in a statement to the *Liverpool Echo*:

'The majority of Negroes at present are discharged soldiers and sailors without employment; in fact some of them are practically starving, work having been refused them on account of their colour ... [We are] unable to obtain work as seafarers. Our goods and our houses have been broken and taken away from us. Some of us have been wounded and lost limbs and eyes fighting for the Empire in which we have the honour to belong.'

Unfortunately, troubling reports of the time show that the local constabulary displayed little motivation to maintain the peace or quell civil unrest, with a sense that the Black seamen had brought the violence on themselves by becoming involved with British women. One experienced police officer was reported saying:

'The people here [in Liverpool] understand the negroes ... They know that most of them are only big children who when they get money like to make a show ... The negroes would not have been touched but for their relations with white women. This caused the entire trouble.'

The message was clear: as long as Black men did not have sexual relations with white women, there would be no violence. So, while there was no *legal* barrier prohibiting interactions between Black men and white women, the social lesson was explicit.

Shifting the blame from the perpetrators of mob atrocity onto the victims was not restricted to the police force. In a letter to *The Times* in 1919, former colonial administrator Sir Ralph Williams wrote:

It is an instinctive certainty that sexual relations between white women and coloured men revolt our very nature ... Large numbers of Black and coloured men have been gathered together in the Mother Country. They are here without their women, and it is not wonderful that their passions should run high after a long period of abstinence. These men now find white women of a certain temperament encouraging their attentions, and allowing themselves to be taken as paramours, or sometimes as wives. What blame to the coloured men if they take advantage of it? And what blame, too, to those white men who, seeing these conditions and loathing them resort to violence?

This 'instinctive certainty' was not something that was an aberrant thought in Western society. The same language that had been used to justify putting Black people onto boats to work as enslaved people under punishment of whip, torture and death, had by the twentieth century morphed into a perverse humanitarianism. While no longer claiming that Black people were mere chattel, there would emerge a supposed divide between 'higher' and 'lower' orders of humanity that would become embedded in the nascent genetic science of the time. Grounded in the eugenicist thinking of Francis Galton, those who were against miscegenation or 'race mixing' positioned themselves as having purely altruistic concerns. The argument went that the offspring of African and white/European relationships were somehow of an inferior stock and anomalous. This was the impetus behind the report sponsored by the Liverpool Association for the Welfare of Half-Caste Children and carried out by Muriel E. Fletcher in 1930, entitled *Report on an Investigation into the Colour Problem in Liverpool and other Parts.*

Backed by the prominent eugenicist Rachel Fleming, the bias in the research is evident even from the title. Fletcher's central thesis is that Black men are responsible for the racial tensions in the city due to their fraternising with white women and that borders must be strengthened to keep them out of Britain. Unsupported claims based in myth about Black sexuality became a crucial tenet of her argument that interracial mixing was damaging to the harmony of the city, claiming that white women 'almost invariably regret their alliance with a coloured man, and realizing that they have chosen a life which is repugnant, become extraordinarily sensitive about their position . . . [Also] their sexual demands impose a continual strain on white women'. She would go on to claim that the only types of women who might choose this 'repugnant lifestyle' were prostitutes, 'younger women who make contacts in the spirit of adventure and are unable to break away', those with illegitimate children and the 'mentally weak'. Those white women who claimed their 'coloured' spouses to be good husbands, Fletcher dismissed as women making excuses for their mistakes.

White women – overwhelmingly white working-class women – do not have agency in Fletcher's mind. She would rather blame the shipping companies who provided lodging for Black sailors, as this appeared to be considerable induce-ment of some kind for the men to settle in this country. Fletcher seems aware of Black British subjects' right to live, settle and work in 'the Motherland', but still feels a deep unease about it, casting doubt on their right to a British passport with unsubstantiated claims of further deception: 'Their claim to British nationality, however, can hardly ever be substantiated, and many are, in fact, Liberians.'

The legitimacy that the Fletcher report was afforded,

despite its flaws in terms of data set, pool size and objectivity, meant that the impact of the so-called research was far wider than just Liverpool. In June of 1930, the *Daily Telegraph* gave notice of the publication of the Fletcher report, describing the findings as evidence of a 'social menace'. Headlines of 'Colour Problem in Britain' and 'Menace of Mixed Unions' stoked fears of 'Black peril' and fomented a moral panic around interracial sexual relationships nationwide. The fear of miscegenation was not limited to journalistic media either. In Keate Weston's novel *London Fog*, from 1934, he writes, 'Black and white mustn't mix, my dear. Not in *that* way. I have seen a good deal of it down at the docks, and believe me, it always ends in tragedy for both. And then – think of the children! It's a crime against nature to bring them into a world that has no place for them.'

The flaws of the report and the flagrant racist assertions within it mean that it is nowadays often dismissed due to our more enlightened understanding of genetics. With the decoding of the human genome showing us that, as humans, we share at least 99.9 per cent of our DNA, there is a desire to ignore our past and the damage it did. Unfortunately, while race is a social, man-made construct, this does not make the effects of racism any less real. The very real impact that the racist language and narratives – such as those contained within the Fletcher report – had, and continue to have, have been cemented into acceptable popular thought.

It was in response to the Labour government's Race Relations Bill of 1968, which would make it illegal to refuse housing, employment or public services to a person on the grounds of colour, race, ethnic or national origins in Britain, that Enoch Powell made his infamous 'Rivers of Blood' speech. Quoting Virgil's *Aeneid*, he declared, 'As I look ahead, I am filled with foreboding; like the Roman, I seem to see the River Tiber foaming with much blood,' calling the bill akin to 'throwing a match onto gunpowder'. Relaying the fears of a constituent, he recounts the man vowing to emigrate from Britain as 'in this country in fifteen or twenty years' time the Black man will have the whip hand over the white man'. Though Edward Heath would sack Powell for stoking racial tensions (against the advice of one Margaret Thatcher, who would herself go on to warn of the dangers of Britain being 'swamped' by Commonwealth migration), a poll at the time said that 75 per cent of the British public were sympathetic to Powell's views. Men who had been culturally primed to assume the warrior role 'even if they weren't at war' would now feel their racial hatred had been emboldened by what *The Times* called 'an evil speech'. Despite this, in response to his sacking, over a thousand people would protest outside the Palace of Westminster with placards bearing 'Back Britain, not Black Britain'. These attitudes, and their widespread nature, would have the potential to cleave my family in two.

My maternal grandfather, John Joseph Ferguson, was born in 1919 in Co. Mayo in the west of Ireland. Coming to London during the Second World War to aid the war effort as a carpenter, he would go on to work on some of the early oil rigs in what is now modern-day United Arab Emirates, travelling the world, working alongside Black and Arab men. They were fine colleagues, and John Joe enjoyed their company, becoming fluent in Arabic – much to the surprise of new acquaintances who weren't expecting a nod of comprehension from the stocky Irishman in response to their native tongue.

As much as he admired them professionally, however, he had also witnessed their racist mistreatment. Black and 'half-caste' British subjects just had a tougher time. He was aware of Britain's own complicated history with Ireland, with signs such as 'No Irish, No Blacks, No Dogs' and 'No Irish need apply' frequently added to accommodation and job advertisements. Perhaps this knowledge is what led to his reaction when his only daughter, his only child, informed him that she wanted him to bless her marriage to a first-generation Nigerian immigrant called Eze. Looking at his nineteen-year-old daughter in front of him, he had an absolute belief, taught to him by society, that by choosing to marry a Black man, and choosing to have 'half-caste' children, she would be setting herself up for a difficult life. This narrative had been fed to him in all forms of media and popular opinion. For John Joe, within the role for which society had primed not just him but all men – that of the warrior 'man of the house' – were all the responsibilities of provider and protector. If he was to be a 'good man', he must ensure that his only child and grandchildren had the best chance in life. A Black son-in-law did not represent the best chance.

Fortunately for me, my parents kept the faith in the face of adverse odds. Given how they first met, it would be easy to think I mean organised, religious, Catholic faith. While this definitely played and still plays a part in their more than three decades of marriage, as a child growing up, I was constantly in awe of their synergy and belief in each other; a knowing glance or a hand placed on the wrist was often more than sufficient to communicate unspoken volumes. The unshakeable faith and belief that they loved each other, and that this was enough to face any challenge, meant that the house I grew up in always felt safe, secure and more than anything, like home.

My mother and father first met at a church group where young people would come together and discuss their faith with the local bishop. It ranks as one of the more chaste origins stories and runs rather counter to the narrative of Black men frequenting nightclubs and bars and picking up young women. My mother, Jacqueline, was a nineteen-year-old student nurse when she met my father, four years her senior and a PhD student at Imperial College London. Within a year of their courtship, with marriage on the cards, so the story goes, my mother informed John Joe about the impending nuptials. His receptiveness to the idea was less than ideal, telling my mother flat out that he did not and would not approve of the marriage.

However he arrived at the decision, and whatever his

justifications were for it, John Joe did not attend my parents' New Year's Day wedding at their parish church, and he forbade his wife from attending also. My mother's walk down the aisle was with her older cousin Jimmy rather than the 'man of the house' she had grown up with. Just over nine months later, my eldest brother Chijioke was born, a honeymoon baby. By this point, perhaps resigned to the situation and the fact that, with my mother being an only child, Chijioke and his future siblings would be John Joe's only grandchildren, there had been a softening in his stance. In-laws met in-laws and our families became intertwined.

My soft memories of bouncing on the sturdy legs of my grandfather, and his kindly face, did not hint at the acrimony and suspicion that he had directed towards my father. Losing John Joe at the age of five, my few memories of him – as with so many memories that relate to my family – are filled with laughter, joy and love. But for many families this is not the case. As the rising global divorce rates show, marriage is no easy thing, yet the safety net of family and friends provides a support that can prove invaluable. My grandmother Teresa would be my first chaperone to Irish music classes while my mother was busy preparing dinner for the rest of the family.

But what if John Joe and Teresa had never softened? What if they had continued to believe the horrendous narratives about 'half-caste' children being somehow inherently less deserving of love, or that interracial marriages were 'unnatural'? Or what if my parents had not been so patient, heartbroken by the lack of support that a parent should give their child? I count myself lucky to have had the presence of both sides of my family, knowing that many of my contemporaries who came from a mixed background had families that could not bring themselves to support their parents' relationship. As grateful as I am that my eldest brother melted my grandparents' hearts – the human panacea that helped unite the in-laws – I find it hard to reconcile my childhood memories of a genteel patriarch with the man who had initially failed to recognise my parents' marriage. I remember John Joe slipping me candied treats as a small boy, blending him in my mind's eye with the actor from the Werther's Original advert. My belated discovery of his former prejudices after his passing left me grappling with the idea that my kind and gentle grandfather had also at one point held sexist and racist beliefs. Could both people exist in one human being, and could that person love and be loved? My parents' seemingly inexhaustible supply of faith and optimism provided space for that love and humanity to exist and grow.

I remember asking my dad about his relationship with his father-in-law and how he reconciled his sense of pride and self-worth with having to wait outside in the car while his wife visited her parents. His response was as matter-of-fact as it was crushing: 'I knew that deep down he loved your mother and that he felt he was doing right by her. I also knew that he hadn't come up with these ideas by himself and that Britain had told him I would not be a good husband or father.'

My grandfather was not present at his daughter's wedding to 'give her away' to my father, but once the reality of a grandchild became tangible, he resumed his role of 'man of the house' by telling my father that he now had to get a proper job and be done with the student life. There were roles that had to be performed and, Black or white, my dad was acutely aware of the parameters that society had placed upon him. Being taught by his parents that education was the great equaliser is perhaps why my parents went to such great pains to ensure that my brothers and I performed academically.

My alma mater was anomalous as a state school, deemed, as it was, worthy of educating the children of the then prime minister, Tony Blair. As a Roman Catholic school, the only entry requirement was that students must attend Mass regularly. There was no equivalent of the 11 Plus exam demanded by grammar schools, and no fees to pay. The philosophy of the headmaster at the time was to give a 'private school education on state school funding'. Latin classes were part of the curriculum, while Saturday morning rugby games against fee-paying schools with grounds three times the size of ours dominated the first half of the school year. Stories of sixth formers trialling for the England team or accepting a place at Oxbridge permeated throughout the school, instilling a sense of entitlement and normality to these achievements. Our ability to compete at this level and the permission that it gave many of us to feel like we belonged in those environments was invaluable. Yet, despite the dizzy heights we aspired to, many Black students would note the almost imperceptible glass ceiling that greeted those whose ambitions rose too high. As with a window that has been cleaned so thoroughly that from a distance you might not perceive its solidity, there seemed no limit to what we could dare to become. The hard reality of the glass, however, would check that progress; the filthiness of the limitation somehow more disappointing when seen up close.

By the summer of my last year at school, I had already decided that I would like to be an actor. Not quite knowing what this meant, other than that I would not be applying to conventional university courses, released a certain amount of educational pressure from my shoulders. For those who wanted to study medicine or apply to Oxbridge, however, there were early applications and the summer was filled with the drafting and redrafting of personal statements to meet the October deadline. One of these candidates happened to be my long-time schooldays confederate and rugby teammate Mark, who, for as long as I'd known him, had had his heart set on studying law at Oxford.

One of a dozen students applying early, he had signed up for a seminar at the beginning of the year on the 'dos and don'ts' of Oxbridge university applications. However, before he had even set foot in the seminar, he was pulled aside. I would only find out the content of the conversation when confronted with a furious but resolute Mark in the sixth form common room. The teacher running the seminar had made it abundantly clear that despite Mark's predicted grades being more than sufficient, and his extra-curricular activities being above and beyond what many of his peers had amassed, he should temper his expectations and consider applying to a more realistic university. I sensed his fury had, on the journey between the seminar and the common room, metamorphosed from a fiery rage into a laser point of resolute determination. 'Just watch, innit.'

I am certain that teacher would never have considered herself a racist. In fact, I believe she self-identified as a 'kind, moral person'. Very few of us are the villains in our own story. Nor do I believe that that one conversation coloured all her actions and made her an immoral person. Unfortunately, as I was learning, life is not and cannot be so binary. We are fully formed, messily nuanced beings who do not exist in a vacuum but are a complex link in a chain of narratives. What I do believe is that, in the precious moment when Mark was daring to dream that he might one day fly with the wings that the school had helped him grow, she had seen fit to diminish him and attempt to clip them. I know that he sat in a room with eleven other students and watched as the ladder they were being offered to climb was pulled away from him, and that through sheer force of self-belief and faith in his own abilities, he would nevertheless achieve his goals.

Just as we were exploring the world and discovering our place in it, the very educators our parents had trusted to help us on our journey would, knowingly or not, attempt to keep us shackled. Fortunately, I knew glass to be a fragile thing. My father would say, '*You* get to decide your place in the world.' For every glass ceiling that I encountered, it would seem to dare me to shatter it.

3

Black Exceptionalism and Bounties

We must accept finite disappointment but never lose infinite hope.

DR MARTIN LUTHER KING JR.

The words of MLK are used (and often misused) across the political spectrum, on both sides of the Atlantic. A faith in humanity's better nature, an 'infinite' supply of hope, is for many marginalised people the only way they can maintain the momentum of swimming upstream against a tide of sexism, racism and all the other prejudices that have become ingrained into our society. The fish that yields to the currents of the river will be carried downstream, and at times it can feel like a mammoth effort just to stay in the same place. It was my parents' infinite hope that gave them the strength to weather the finite disappointment of a temporary familial schism. What Dr King captures so succinctly is that, while the momentum of the ills of society is demoralising, progress *can* be made and that hope and faith in humanity's intrinsic beneficence would bring us there. The symbol of that hope and sign of that progress were arguably never more sharply felt than on US Election Day, November 2008.

My parents and I gathered around the TV in the living room that Tuesday evening, supplies of chocolate Hobnobs and McVitie's Digestives at the ready for what promised to be a marathon evening. The news was dripping in at an agonisingly glacial pace. My father drifted in and out, a cup of tea in his hand. His running commentary and observations exuded a gentle cynicism about the unfolding events, tempered by his own lived experience of frequent disappointments. My mother, half asleep on the sofa, was an equally fickle sentinel, waking periodically to my shouts of excitement as I saw another state turn blue. For my part I stayed the course, undeterred by the five-hour time difference. My eighteen-year-old body was too high on optimism to let my eyes rest. It was still dark outside in the early hours of the morning when the first predictions started coming in. I called my father into the living room, my heart fit to burst. When, at four in the morning, US news networks unanimously declared Barack Obama the winner, I felt a euphoric release; a thousand sentiments felt but unable to be put into words. I oscillated between giddy, overtired excitement and stunned disbelief at the seismic importance of it all.

A century-and-a-half after slavery was abolished, and fewer than fifty years after Martin Luther King led the march on Washington DC, Barack Obama, the first Black president of the *Harvard Law Review* and Senator for the state of Illinois, had been elected 44th President of the United States of America. For so long perceived with a degree of condescension by their British neighbours because of their outwardly contentious relationship with race, the US seemed to be signalling that it was ready to confront its demons. States like Indiana and North Carolina that had traditionally provided the Republican Party with Electoral College votes had come out in favour of this first-time senator. He was the first president born in Hawaii, but most importantly to the millions of Americans who had just voted in a new president, he had a Black father. A Black African father. During his 'More Perfect Union' campaign speech, which many pundits would see as the moment he solidified his support among undecided white voters across the country, Obama would reference his layered, complex upbringing as a Black man in the US.

I am the son of a Black man from Kenya and a white woman from Kansas. I was raised with the help of a white grandfather who survived a Depression to serve in Patton's Army during World War II and a white grandmother who worked on a bomber assembly line at Fort Leavenworth while he was overseas. I've gone to some of the best schools in America and lived in one of the world's poorest nations. I am married to a Black American who carries within her the blood of slaves and slaveowners – an inheritance we pass on to our two precious daughters. I have brothers, sisters, nieces, nephews, uncles and cousins of every race and every hue, scattered across three continents, and for as long as I live, I will never forget that in no other country on Earth is my story even possible.

The hope that my parents had for me was that I might be able to 'decide my place in the world'. Against all the odds, a Black man had been elected the most powerful man in the world by a nation that had wrestled with the idea of race since its inception. No matter what policy accomplishments Obama would achieve over the next term or two, nothing could change the immutable fact of his election on that November morning. The US had crossed the Rubicon; the story had now shifted forever. The unlikely coalescence of dissatisfaction with the previous administration, growing disillusionment with US foreign policy and Obama's unusual gift for oratory set the stage for a chapter that ran counter to the country's complicated history with anti-Black racism and discrimination.

His election seemed to tell a counter-narrative to the one that had coursed through US history for centuries, that optimists willed themselves to believe; one which spoke to the innate humanity of Americans and somehow beyond. Something had happened that transcended age, creed and most importantly colour, and it had shifted not only US but global politics. Rather than shy away from the mythos surrounding his position as the post-racial totemic saviour the country had long sought, the presidential candidate leaned into it, remarking weeks before his election, 'Contrary to the rumours you have heard, I was not born in a manger. I was actually born on Krypton and sent here by my father, Jor-el, to save the planet Earth.' A charming and pithy quip; I doubt Obama knew then that it would be questions around his heritage that would launch his successor into the forefront of US politics and an unexpectedly successful tilt at The White House.

Donald Trump's peddling of questions around Obama's birth, and as such the legitimacy of his presidency, would plant the seeds necessary for Trump's political ambitions to be realised. The US Constitution declares that any presidential candidate must be born in the United States. The 'birther' conspiracy, as it came to be known, was a flagrant racist attack and would prove the kryptonite with which to attack Obama's legacy. In a world where millions, myself included, saw him as unlikely a superhero as Clark Kent, but a superhero nonetheless, for millions of others he would always be defined and limited by his race.

But on that November morning, as my parents headed up the stairs to the sounds of Sam Cooke playing through the house, I heard Obama's refrain emanating from the TV: 'Yes We Can.' My faith had been renewed.

*

'For you to get half as far, you'll have to work twice as hard.'

My father was told this by his parents, and he in turn told me. This was not unique to the Ugoala family. All of my Black friends recall being told similar axioms from the lips of their parents, aunties and uncles or some other concerned adult while they were growing up. Unfortunately, their fears were not unfounded. According to a 2009 study from NatCen Social Research, job applicants with a white-sounding name were 74 per cent more likely to get a positive response than those with an ethnic minority name. The role models that I grew up with – from my father to Ian Wright, Muhammad Ali to Dwayne Johnson, Sidney Poitier to Barack Obama – represented the plurality of Black masculinity. Their unifying quality was excellence in their field. Whether it was on the football field or running track, wrestling ring or Grammy stage, there was no shortage of Black men that demonstrated their ability to excel despite the institutional barriers in their way. Closer to home, my father was a sterling example of defying the expectations that society might have for Black men.

My father arrived in London in the 1960s as a child refugee accompanied by my grandmother fleeing the Nigeria-Biafran war that was raging in the aftermath of the UK granting Nigeria its independence. When he first arrived, he was suffering, as many Biafran children were, from the severe form of malnutrition called kwashiorkor, characterised by a swollen gut. With the dawn of global television reporting, the victims of the effects of enforced famine and food blockades – which had seen as many as a thousand children a day dying of starvation – were seen by millions globally, and significantly by viewers in the West.

The Nigerian colonel Benjamin Adekunle maintained that the denial of food to Biafrans was a necessary strategy, declaring: 'If the children must die first, then that is too bad, just too bad.' For my grandparents, those terms were unacceptable, and my father was one of the lucky few that could make safe passage to London. My grandmother Lucy was training in London on a secondment when the civil war first broke out. Seeing an opportunity to volunteer with the British Red Cross as part of the Biafran Airdrop that would bring humanitarian aid to the starving children in the middle of the conflict, she dived in headlong, gathering her children to her on the return flight back to the UK.

This chance that had been granted to my family was not one that my grandparents would allow to be scuppered by something as trivial as racism. To hear my father speak today, you would be forgiven for assuming he was a London native, born and raised. The only time I ever heard the Nigerian lilt return was when he answered the house phone and recognised the voice at the other end of the line as being that of a friend or relative from 'back home'. He had barely been in the British education system a decade when he won a place to study at Imperial College London, where he would be awarded a PhD in Plasma Physics. My grandparents, like many immigrants to Britain, believed that education and money were the two insulations to racism in this country.

Lacking familial wealth, a doctorate would have to do. He was cognisant of the double standards at play and the patience he would have to employ to circumnavigate them. He would often say, 'Give them no excuse not to hire you.' I was fifteen years old before I first heard my father swear – the news of the loss of a family member jolting him out of his usual propriety. When my mother told me one day that he had considered becoming a priest before he had met her, it made perfect sense. Teetotal, because he 'never really saw the appeal' of alcohol, the patience and selflessness he had at his disposal seemed saint-like. He would need it.

I had just entered my teens when the company car that my dad was entitled to had to be put in for repair. My brothers and I were suitably in awe when we came outside to see him driving the black BMW that had been provided as a courtesy replacement; the company he was working for needed him at head office that month and he would be doing a lot of driving. With the capacity to hold multiple CDs at any one time, it felt like the height of luxury and style to be able to choose from more than a hundred different songs. My father rarely splashes out on the more extravagant niceties in life, so this forced imposition of a luxury vehicle felt, to our eyes, like a welcome indulgence.

After less than a fortnight of driving it, however, he requested an alternative vehicle and was issued a more modest family car. Outraged at not being able to flick between our favourite tracks, we raised the issue with our mum. The familiar tinge of sadness in her eyes did not bode well, as she explained that Dad had been stopped by the police five times in the previous fortnight. Pulling him over, they would interrogate him about the ownership of the vehicle, his documentation and the details of his journey. Having been a passenger and map reader countless times for my father, I was aware of his adherence to the rules. The depressing realisation that he was being pulled over for presumably driving the 'wrong type of car' and not for any legal infraction still rankles with me. His response to the police officers however was always a Michelle Obama-esque, 'When they go low, we go high.' I would later enquire of my father, did he not want to call them out on the blatant profiling? His reply: 'I wouldn't give them the satisfaction of seeing me angry.'

My dad has always been a huge fan of Sidney Poitier. Outside of tired tropes, substantial roles for Black actors have been few and far between. The Bahamian-American actor took special pains to take on roles that challenged negative stereotypes about Black men, fully aware that he was one of the few actors of African descent being cast in leading roles at the time. Each time *In The Heat of the Night* happened to be on terrestrial television on a Sunday afternoon, it was a given that it would be the family entertainment for the following couple of hours. And every time *that* scene came on the screen, my father would stop whatever he was doing and pause to watch it.

In the film, Poitier plays a Black homicide detective. When, in the investigation of a murder, a wealthy local takes against the tone Poitier's detective uses in questioning, he slaps him across the face. Without missing a beat, Sidney Poitier returns the slap with interest, stunning the suspect into silence. I say Poitier rather than Tibbs because – as urban legend has it, told to me by Dad and echoed by countless others over the years – the retaliatory slap was improvised and a moment of righteous payback for every Black man who had wanted to lash out in response to racist acts of violence but had feared the retribution. The truth of the matter, as with much of Poitier's life, was more thought-through and calculated. In discussing the scene, the director, Norman Jewison, would later say, 'A Black man had never slapped a white man in an American film. We broke that taboo.' Vicarious catharsis by way of watching this exceptional Black man retaliate physically, however, was the closest my father would come to violence, so alien is it to him and his sensibilities.

There is a line of scripture that seems to inform much of my father's outlook on life: 'To whom much is given, much will be required.' The sanguine attitude that he was capable of employing was matched beat for beat by my mother, Jackie. It was their deep capacity for patience, coupled with their selflessness, that encouraged my parents to become foster carers. Not long after they had my eldest brother, Chi, they began fostering children from a local council. Some would stay with us for barely a day and some would become integrated parts of the family, staying for months and in some cases years. At the time, my parents were anomalous in being one of the few interracial families that were fostering. So, over the next two decades, I would meet, live with, bond, fight and grow to love children from all walks of life, notably several other young Black men who would have their own rude awakenings about the lack of privilege being born Black in Britain would afford them. I was taught both by my family and my foster siblings that the world I was growing up in was not designed with me in mind, whether that was in terms of education, employment or the justice system. In my parents' minds, being excellent in my chosen field was one of my first tools in keeping safe, not just financially, but bodily.

My desire for bodily safety played out most notably in my voice. From a young age I learned that modifying my voice – or 'code switching' – to sound more stereotypically white would make those in majority-white spaces more receptive to me. The ease with which my father would switch back into his native Igbo dialect when speaking to family members back home demonstrated the duality of his experience. Yet, despite our familial embrace of Nigerian culture, the language, which in many cultures is the primary gateway to understanding fully the foundations on which a culture is built, was something that was not given priority – to me or my brothers.

The badge of bilingual is lauded and praised in society for certain languages and not others. So, as I struggled to master the declensions and conjugations in French and Latin, my father-tongue fell to the wayside. I am not alone among my friends in being a second-generation Nigerian who has belatedly taken up language classes as an adult to further connect with my roots. Where I saw freedom in my father's ability to switch between languages, I also felt a sense of being untethered, without an anchor in a restless sea of British culture that was constantly trying to define me and place me in a box. When I was with my north London friends, or some of my older foster siblings, I felt free to express myself however *I* chose: freestyle rapping and beatboxing in the N1 shopping centre in Angel or chilling on a park bench eating a bargain meal deal from the boss man at the local chicken shop. My accent, hobbies and even my taste in music felt authentic. But when I was dealing with choirmasters or casting directors, I knew that the 'urban quality' of my accent would be perceived as a lack of refinement. Making a conscious effort to conform one term, I witnessed the subtle degree of leniency teachers gave to me because I began to fit their preconceived idea of what a polite boy would sound and look like. My thoughts turned back to my hair and my internal exclusion for having it too short. Did my ability to be a vocal chameleon betray my Blackness? Was I justifying the insult thrown at me by Black peers at school, that I was a 'Bounty' – Black on the outside and white on the inside, like the chocolate bar? Or could my Blackness be individual, defined by me and me alone?

Growing up Black in London, it wasn't just the school or justice system that heaped performative expectations on your shoulders. After walking into the living room and finding me practising scales on the piano, one of my foster brothers, James, who had been with us only a few days, fired the insult at me. Asking him why I couldn't like classical music, his reply was, 'Because that's gay shit. You're meant to be into garage.'

My parents were acutely aware of the intricacies of raising three Black sons. Like many parents of Black boys, they had watched the aftermath of Stephen Lawrence's murder unfold with horror. Though London's Metropolitan Police was labelled as 'institutionally racist', it did little to change behaviours and attitudes at a systemic level. I was the same age as Damilola Taylor when the young Nigerian boy was murdered in a stairwell of a south London estate days before his eleventh birthday. Though I heard and felt I had heeded their warnings about 'not drawing attention to yourself', my naïve sense of imperviousness persisted until I was confronted with the murder of Anthony Walker. Reading the news report while lying on my bed, I found myself rocked by the events for weeks. Just eighteen years of age, he was accosted by two men, unprovoked. When he tried to avoid the confrontation and walk with his girlfriend to another bus stop to escape their attention, they would shout, 'Walk, nigger, walk' after him before pursuing him and driving an ice axe into his skull. It proved a harsh reminder that sometimes in Britain, 'being Black' is drawing attention to yourself; you can't always define who you are in the world. I was still figuring out what that meant as a young Black man.

*

One ever feels his two-ness, – an American, a
Negro; two souls, two thoughts, two unreconciled
strivings; two warring ideals in one dark body,
whose dogged strength alone keeps it from being
torn asunder

William Edward Burghardt Du Bois

The conflict Du Bois is describing is the desire that Black people feel to be seen as individuals, set against their awareness that they do not exist in a vacuum. Western society has been told and regurgitated anti-Black narratives for centuries. It is the widespread insidiousness of those narratives that often creates the commonality of experience felt by members of the African diaspora. The divide of oceans or landmasses is often bridged by the words of writers, poets and artists capable of expressing the sense of displacement felt by Black people in a racist society. While I didn't grow up in Compton, California, Coolio's lyrics from the soundtrack to *Dangerous Minds* spoke to me and made me feel seen, known and understood in the visceral way that great art should.

It was hearing me recite these lyrics through the wall of my bedroom that brought James to my door one evening.

'What do you know about Coolio?' he asked, as he stood in the doorway.

I shrugged. 'It's just a banger,' I deflected, self-consciously.

'Is that you, yeah? Okay, okay,' he chortled. 'You should still be listening to garage though, rather than that gay piano shit.'

'It's not gay shit. Plus,' I said, smug as all hell, 'who said I don't know about garage?'

Presenting him with the blue album case of *Pure Garage 1*, I saw the look on his face go from patronising to bemusement.

'Ratings! Nah, I see you. We need to get you an MC name. Let me think.' He presented his fist welcomingly, waiting for me to spud him in return. Softening, I obliged.

For James – or Big J, as the boys from his estate in Stoke Newington knew him – his narrative was linked to Avirex jackets and Nike New Era hats that acted as his uniform. The culture he saw representing him and his aspirations was that of the garage MCs of the early '00s, who had seen the recognition of their rapping talent yield not only financial success, but also respect from their peers. His clothes communicated status; his fresh fade from the Black barbershop spoke of self-respect; and appreciating garage, with its honest urban narratives, was an empowered ownership of the grim realities he faced in life. His contemporaries put their talent into documenting and reflecting the life they knew in their music; and the fact that it was a harsher reality than I had experienced as a young Black man irked him on some level. Perhaps this is why I didn't feel able to call out his homophobic dismissal of playing the piano. Or maybe it was that my fifteen-year-old self did not have the ability to recall great Black pianists such as Ray Charles, Stevie Wonder or Nina Simone. Either way, looking back now, I feel ire that either one of us felt that the piano wasn't something

Black people were *supposed* to do, or indeed that being a gay pianist was somehow wrong. But in James's version of masculinity, young Black men weren't allowed to listen to the *wrong kinds* of music. Nor be gay. For us, boys like him and me, our role was simple: get money and draw gash.

Teenage brains are so absorbent that it was only several years later, once I was more acquainted with the female body, that I realised that 'drawing gash', which had come to mean garnering the interest of a young woman and successfully exchanging numbers with the intention of a date, derived its meaning from female genitalia. Young men, it seems, were not too interested in the nuance of describing the female experience, and it wasn't uncommon to witness friends of mine attempting to woo complete strangers on the street. Bragging about the amount of mobile phone numbers that had been collected seemed to be the most important metric of success rather than establishing any particular connection with a woman. Women were disposable and not to be connected with on an emotional level. No place was this rhetoric more apparent than in Dizzee Rascal's debut single 'I Luv U'. Boasting about his unwillingness to perform oral sex on his female partner, he proclaims that he isn't a 'bowcat'. Dizzee constantly frames the woman in question as a 'whore' who has most likely had sex with six people in a row. Bowcat would be thrown around the playground as an insult, as if the idea of female pleasure is inherently emasculating to men. The demonisation and flat-out disregard of women and female sexuality was extolled and rewarded, and women were seen as a means to an end: namely status.

The centuries-old trope of men in the warrior role continues to be repeated on London streets as young men try to live up to outdated models of what it is to be a successful young man. The inherent violence of teaching young men that they are entitled to a woman's body if they say or do the right thing, that 'no' does not in fact mean 'no', and that persistence will be rewarded – a dangerous notion reinforced and fed to boys of all backgrounds in wider media – means that women will often invent a fictional boyfriend so that they might feel safer when approached. In the experience of my peers, it would not be an uncommon sight for a girl to rebuff a man's advance only to be met with accusations of being 'stoosh', 'frigid' or 'butterz anyways'. In framing sexual interaction as a 'battle of the sexes', there is an unspoken acceptance of violence: conqueror and conquered, victor and defeated. Learning from our peers and the wider culture around us, the journey from prize of the Disney prince to reward-in-waiting at the bus stop was not a long one. For James, like many boys his age, Black or otherwise, anybody who didn't meet these expectations was seen as a threat, an attempted subversion of his status by refusing to play by the rules of the game.

For many young Black boys who have been punished, excluded and unsupported throughout their schooling process, other than success with the opposite sex, money is one of the few indicators of success and status. The Nike hat collections and Evisu jeans of my teenage years were signposts to wealth, and as such a source of pride. The line between actual and perceived wealth is often so fine as to be almost indistinguishable. The risk that might need to be undertaken to achieve that wealth is deemed worth it, even if it means criminal activity. At the time of writing, the most expensive fee-paying school in the country charges upwards of £42,000 a year. This feels like an astronomical amount of money to invest in a child's life chances. That is until it is compared with the £61,000 a year that the government spends incarcerating each young male offender. The effect of pulling funding from youth services, leading to a 51 per cent drop in the overall number of youth centres supported by English local authorities since 2011, means the political posturing about trying to tackle youth crime rings very hollow. For many, youth centres serve as safe environments in the community and their defunding and lack of support from successive governments is perceived by many as telling with regard to the futures of young adults.

Javed Khan, the Chief Executive of Barnado's, the children's charity, responded to the figures. 'Taking away youth workers and safe spaces in the community contributes to a "poverty of hope" among young people who see little or no chance of a positive future.' By the time many young Black boys have fallen through the net of the education system and run afoul of the justice system, the rates of recidivism are depressingly high: 68 per cent of children released from custody reoffend within the year. When this is coupled with disproportionate targeting by the police – Black people are more than nine times more likely to be stopped and searched – the vicious cycle of a combative relationship between members of the Black community and the justice system shows little sign of improving.

Black boys are disproportionately represented within the criminal justice system, and figures obtained under freedom of information requests by Transform Justice show over 60 per cent of children on remand in London are Black. From the Macpherson Report of 1999 to the Lammy Review in 2017, the recommendations of how to improve race relations with the police have been largely ignored, with yet another racial equality review, headed by Tony Sewell, raising eyebrows due to his scepticism of the existence of institutional racism, announced by Boris Johnson in 2020 in response to the Black Lives Matter protests. The suspicion around the report by the Commission on Race and Ethnic Disparities would be well-founded after the Commission went on to make the unsubstantiated claim that there was no institutional racism in Britain, instead citing 'pessimism', 'linguistic inflation' and 'emotion' as grounds to distrust and deligitimise the data and narratives associated with racism and racial discrimination. Human rights experts from the UN would excoriate the report, saying it 'categorically rejects and condemns the analysis and findings', and called it 'an attempt to normalise white supremacy'.

Time after time, it seems these reviews and reports are commissioned and yet the underlying problems persist, leaving the impression that consecutive governments are more concerned about being seen to act rather than taking quantifiable, tangible action to address the issues. One commissioner who contributed to the report would lambast its rushed delivery, completed a mere seven months after their initial convening, where both the Lammy Review and the Macpherson Report would take eighteen months to conclude, accusing the government of 'bending' the work of its commission to fit 'a more palatable' political narrative. Perhaps my lack of faith in who the police exist to protect and serve might be why, when I found myself most in need of police assistance, my immediate instinct wasn't to rely on them.

It was dark by the time I headed home alone after a drama class at the Young Actors Theatre Islington – formerly the Anna Scher Theatre School in Angel. I was aware that my school uniform was obviously not that of any of the local schools, so I had stripped off my school tie in an attempt to make myself less conspicuous. A healthy fifteen stone and hitting six foot, I felt safe walking home alone, but for some reason my usual group of bus journey companions weren't at class, and the air felt pregnant with tension as I headed to the bus stop. Hubris, however, had got the better of me. Although I spotted the four teenagers ahead of me, by the time I made to cross the road to avoid walking past them, one of them intercepted me.

'Heyo, PUSSYHOLE! Where you going, blud? What you

got for me?' A faux smile flashed across his face as he began to reach into my pockets.

I'd heard this script before, and James had warned me that I couldn't be taken for a fool; my bark would have to tell these youths the bite wasn't worth the risk.

I gripped his wrist as I stared him in the eye. 'Who you calling Pussyhole?'

'Rah. So you think you're a big man, yeah?' He stopped to gauge me before he continued. 'Who'd you roll with?'

At this point I was surrounded, and while I didn't have much on me other than a rudimentary mobile phone, it was mine and not for the taking.

'You man really wanna come for the Legends of Stoke? Are you dumb?'

'LOS?'

'Big J is my big brother. You man really wanna go?' I paused. They assessed.

'Nah, it's cool, rudeboi. Just didn't recognise you in this neeky uniform. Spud me.'

I paused. We fist-bumped.

'It's bless.'

As they let me pass and carry on walking, my heart pounded. It was stupid. It was reckless. I had gambled and my perceived proximity to what these boys deemed 'acceptable' was enough that they did not feel the urge to call my bluff. At the height of the postcode wars, during which gangs of predominantly young men would challenge or attack and rob other young people they didn't recognise if they came from the 'wrong' postcode, it felt like once a week another story would flash across the evening newspapers littering the train carriages of my journey home from school, of another young boy being assaulted and killed during a mugging. I had risked my life. My heart thundered as I continued on my way to the bus stop. Each of the boys' faces was etched into my mind. All five of us Black boys thrust into a warrior scenario where the only solution seemed to be that of violence. My chameleon-like ability to code-switch and seemingly 'switch off' my whiteness made me less vulnerable. My perceived Blackness made me less of a target. In the world James navigated, he felt a performative version of Black masculinity kept him safe. Compromising that by listening to 'white music' or engaging in scholarly pursuits hadn't been presented to him as a convincing defence against a racist society. As a young Black man, he had been taught that wasn't a viable option for him, especially after the school system had failed him. While my ability to flip accents safeguarded me in that particular moment, the imposter syndrome I felt in certain spaces was always there – and never more so than in my early dating life.

It is no secret that dating and puberty make for an at times heady, confusing, elating mix of glorious highs and ventricle-shattering lows. My experience was no different. Fumbling around in the dark in the desperate attempt to ascertain what girls *really* want was a rather Frankensteinian affair. The days of Page 3 were behind us, surpassed by the erotica-lite agony aunt pages near the sport section and the men's lifestyle magazines that boasted knowledge of female anatomy. Braggadocio and one-upmanship slowly morphed into a crescendo-ing peer pressure as, one by one, members of my friendship group began to lose their virginity. Train journeys and lunchrooms became hives of gossip as we regaled each other with escapades from the weekend's house parties. Before long, it was distinctly uncool to be a virgin.

Perhaps that was why I didn't miss a beat when one of the rugby team asked me how many girls I'd slept with. The equating of me as one of the cool kids, and the cool kids as having had sex, meant that the 'four!' that I blurted out felt almost honest. From the age of fifteen, the coaches that ferried the rugby teams to away matches often included all the older year groups together. Eager-eared and keen to be 'in' with the in-crowd, we would imitate the racy and smutty chants about sexual conquests taught to us by the 1st XV, ready to join in whenever called upon. Learning as many verses to the chants as possible was essential in case one of the sixth formers from the 1st XV nominated you to join in on what would now euphemistically be called 'locker room talk'. Taking the form of 'call and response', the coach would be full of teenage boys egging each other on before a game in the spirit of togetherness, with the price high if you stumbled on your words, as I would find out.

The 1st XV captain, Thomas, was leading the chants and we were all joining in.

I used to work in Chicago, in an old department store
I used to work in Chicago, but I don't work
    there anymore
THOMAS: *A woman came into the store looking for*
    a computer.
ALL OF US: *A computer from the store?*
THOMAS: *A computer she wanted, my hard*
    drive she got!

We all guffawed with laughter, even though we had heard these punchlines countless times before.

. . . But I don't work there anymore.
THOMAS: *Alright, Obi, you're up*

The entire coach turned to me, waiting expectantly to hear me draw from one of a plethora of seedy gags. Initiating the younger boys was a rarity, and I could see the expectation from my own teammates wanting me to do well. But I had been caught off guard.

'A woman . . . A woman came into the store for . . .'

And just like that, the moment was gone; the ball dropped. I had forty-odd boys pointing and jeering at me: 'FAIL!' 'FLOPPED IT!' 'CHOKE!' The rod of correction hit hard. Next time, I would know what to say. Next time, I would get it right.

Before long I would nail down my position as the 1st XV number 8, and my friends and I would be leading the chants, miseducating the boys in the years below us as the cycle continued, maintaining the vulgar tradition. In those male-only environments, we taught each other to be crude conquerors of the opposite sex. Our coaches and teachers would roll their eyes, accepting it as part of the culture. Boys will be boys. But oh, how we longed to not be anymore! So much so, that when my first serious girlfriend posed the same question to me as we texted back and forth about me staying over, the same lie slipped from my fingers. The social dread of being perceived as sexually inexperienced emboldened my mendacity. Though I had undertaken thorough research into the matter, I had no idea what was about to happen. This was my first time staying at my girl-friend's house. It was my first time in her bedroom. It was my first time.

A year older than me and educated at an expensive south London private school, she had recently broken up with her long-term boyfriend. After meeting at a Saturday music course where we sang a duet of 'The Lady is a Tramp', the flirtation graduated from MSN Messenger nudges and hour-long conversations, to texting, to kisses on an ice rink in Queensway after bowling, to this moment – and finally to being welcomed into her free house. Her parents were at a function in the country.

Armed with a bottle of port that had been pilfered from my parents' drinks store, knowing that the lack of frequent alcoholic consumption in our house meant this was effectively a victimless crime, we loaded *The Notebook* into the DVD player, valiantly attempting to uphold the pretence that the very thing we had spent hours late at night discussing and imagining was definitely not going to happen. Our nerves were slowly conquered by underappreciated, totally inappropriate fortified wine, and soon enough small talk began to peter out. So it was that Ryan Gosling and Rachel McAdams became muted witnesses to my deflowering.

'Esme told me that it was totally different with a Black guy, but I never expected ... I mean ... phew!'

What? How do I reply to this? She thinks you weren't a virgin. Keep up the pretence. It's fine.

'Have you never got with a Black guy before?'

'No. But now I'm wondering what took me so bloody long!'

What? How do I reply to this? (In case it wasn't obvious by now, she was white.)

'I'd definitely call myself Celtic. I've for sure got Irish in me. And my grandfather has a castle just over the border in Scotland.'

My non-whiteness, or more specifically, my Blackness, was something that I suddenly realised had currency with her. The colour of my skin, which had been the cause of my teen discomfort in so many other situations, from the racial epithets of opponents on the rugby pitch to the ignorant comments of teachers at school, and had even on more than one occasion led to physical assault, had now become my 'trump card' to this girl who I had spent the past few months getting to know. This would be the first time I would be taught in person, reinforced over the following decade, that when it came to dating, playing the infamous 'race card' could give me an advantage none of my white classmates could have. The complexity of my feelings around what it meant to be *truly* Black was at the centre of my imposter syndrome. How did I wrestle with my race being an arbitrary thing that made me a viable partner? After all, it was just another physical attribute, much like my hair, height or build? So why did the words sting, coming from someone I had just shared such an intimate moment with?

The sense of imposter syndrome would not abate any time soon. Not long after our port-fuelled rendezvous, I was invited to dinner with her parents at their house.

'Don't worry if my dad gives you a hard time. He's just protective of his princess,' she warned, the day she extended the invite. This did little to assuage my fears. Discussing my growing neurosis in the lunchroom, my white friends couldn't understand my anxiety. My Black friends, however, had a different take. Mark tried to reassure me:

'Dude, don't worry about it. We're "Access Blacks". You sound posher than the Queen, sing Mozart every Saturday and you're captain of the rugby team. I'm getting straight As, volunteer at the local primary school teaching kids how to read during free lessons and I'm gonna study law at Oxford.'

I hated how much sense it made; that there was something

about my work ethic, extracurricular activities or the way I spoke that could counterbalance my race and make me more palatable. And yet this was precisely what those films where Sidney Poitier carried himself with exceptional grace and dignity would show me.

In 1967, the same year that he starred in *In The Heat of the Night*, the classic *Guess Who's Coming to Dinner* was released. The movie, about an interracial couple who decide to get married, came out just three weeks before the US Supreme Court, in Loving v. Virginia, struck down racial miscegenation laws as unconstitutional. The film, a spiritual forefather of the Academy Award-winning *Get Out*, is blunt about dealing with the societal challenges that the couple will face. When Poitier's potential father-in-law-to-be first hears about the impending nuptials, he phones his assistant, enraged, asking her to do a background check on the Black man currently sat in his drawing room. The softening of both him and his wife as they listen to the unfeasibly long list of achievements that Poitier's Dr John Prentice has amassed is telling. Graduating top of his class from Johns Hopkins University, lecturing as a university professor and spending three years as assistant director of the World Health Organisation would make for an overachieving son-in-law in the present day, let alone in the 1960s with all the hurdles he would have had to overcome.

Once more my father's words came back to me: 'You will have to work twice as hard.' Perhaps that was why the trepidation I felt in meeting my girlfriend's parents was heightened. I was neither a medical doctor, nor did I have a PhD from Imperial. I was not Black and excellent, just a struggling teenager who liked to sing and play rugby. Would my ability to code-switch, blend in and somehow modify my Blackness soften my girlfriend's parents? As it turned out, I wouldn't have the chance to find out.

Being dumped by your first serious girlfriend is never likely to be a joyous experience. But I can still remember the cavalier look on her face and the sheer unapologetic nature with which she delivered it.

'I just don't see us as a serious thing.'

'Oh, I'm sorry for inviting myself to your parents for dinner, then,' I quipped back pettily. I hadn't mastered the art of being broken up with just yet.

'Look, I've just got a lot going on. I've got exams coming up. I wanted to experiment before I went to uni, and we've had fun. It was either date a girl or a Black guy.'

Yet again I was left speechless. I stared back at her like a scolded puppy. I wonder perhaps if in that moment she saw through my façade of being an experienced Lothario. The offhand nature with which she explained her motivation made me feel like it was the most obvious thing in the world and that I was a fool to expect anything less. In her mind, experimenting meant the targeted aim of sleeping with a Black man, just as her friend Esme had advised her to do. It did not matter how excellent I was as a man; in her eyes, I was an experiment before she went to university and now

I had served my purpose. The wisdom that comes with age grants me a more sanguine perspective looking back, but in all honesty, my fragile male ego was wounded. Trying to not let it show, I responded with platitudes about how I 'totally understood' and 'who knows what the future holds', but we would not have a fairy-tale ending like Rachel McAdams and Ryan Gosling, spanning decades. I was a brief dalliance, an itch to be scratched, and I had now satisfied her curiosity. Rather than dispel my insecurities about failing to meet expectations in being suitable enough to meet her family, it would compound my teenage anxiety that perhaps if I had done something different or compromised myself more, I might have been good enough.

My father's sense of exceptionalism, his self-belief, had empowered him. Yet I couldn't help but feel the constant high standards that he imposed on himself, which required that he filter himself through an acknowledged sense of what was deemed 'acceptable Blackness', was a response to the racist narratives around Black men that he had been taught and had internalised. This was also *limiting*, and I instinctively rebelled against my father's demand for excellence. Not because I didn't believe that I could reach it, but because it felt so at odds with the promise that had been made to the country's white population. In the words of Du Bois, I didn't want to be aware of my otherness. I wanted freedom to be myself. The burden and weight of responsibility that my father felt was one that would pass on to me.

It is the guilt that comes with knowledge, true knowledge of how lucky you are to be in the position that you are. This wisdom brings with it an implied moral duty, to pass the ladder back down because 'to whom much is given, much is required'. That burden was not isolated to our familial experience alone, as one of the final, heart-wrenching scenes in *Guess Who's Coming to Dinner* would attest.

In trying to make Dr Prentice understand that he is making a mistake in his eyes by marrying a white woman and, after all his achievements, risking being a disappointment to him, his father chastises him with a reminder of his own sacrifices as a mailman, recalling the years of work and hours he put in, foregoing gifting his wife the most basic of presents so that his son might have every opportunity in the world. The sense of something owed and a debt to be repaid is a fractious, double-edged sword. On the one hand, I saw the opportunities that lay before me, and the harsher realities of life and potential traumas I was shielded from. Yet on the other, I was deeply aware of the luck of my situation and the responsibility I bore to rise above the fray and make something of myself *despite* the obstacles that lay in my way.

Even as I considered Dr Prentice, with his unfeasible job with the WHO, I felt a disconnect. Despite the superficial similarities he bore with my father as an intelligent, handsome, eloquent Black man, he did not feel familiar. For a film made in the middle of the civil rights struggle in the US, Poitier's character seemed neutered and apolitical. This was no accident. The director, Stanley Kramer, later commented that he made Prentice a paragon of virtue in order to force audiences to confront the issue of colour prejudice directly. 'Hell, we deliberately made the situation perfect, and for only one reason. If you take away all the other motives for not getting married, then you leave only one question: will Tracy forbid the marriage because Poitier's a Negro? That is the only issue, and we deliberately removed all other obstacles to focus on it.'

In doing so, however, he created a character that was out of place within the social context he was in. Kramer deliberately flattened the character of Prentice, not believing that his audiences would be able to navigate the complexity of a three-dimensional Black man. Perhaps this is why Dr Prentice is so chaste and virtuous. His fiancée Joanna laughs off the idea he would have pre-marital sex; he will only be married with his prospective in-laws' blessing, and the only kiss he shares is in the mirror of the taxi that collects them from the airport. His only other overt signalling of his sexuality is his teasing of Joanna that he is interested in her Black maid, seemingly to imply that he is not solely interested in white women.

Decades later, sat in that café in north London opposite my now ex-girlfriend, I was suddenly acutely aware that no matter how much I compromised myself, sometimes it would never be enough. I did not fit into James's idea of what a Black man should be, nor did Mark's notion of 'Access Black' sit well on my skin. No amount of money or education would suddenly be able to singlehandedly alter centuries of notions of what a Black man should be. Yet that is precisely what Kramer posits.

In the final scene, after lashing out at his father, Dr Prentice says, 'Dad, you're my father. I'm your son. I love you. I always have and I always will. But you think of yourself as a coloured man. I think of myself as a man.' This sentiment, though borne of the same spirit as Dr King's wonderful words of optimism, or the hope that brought Obama to The Oval Office, is at best naïve and at worst dangerous. It lulls us into a false sense of security. By us, I mean all of us – Black and white people alike, across the globe. By modelling and centring our idea of what is a 'good man' in one that is steeped in whiteness, we risk absolving ourselves of the work that must be done. It places the onus on Black people to be chaste 'paragons of virtue' rather than normal people. It can also cause parents to enforce double standards on their Black sons because they do not trust the racist society they live in to nurture their child, as they might if they were white. For those who do not manage to be deemed acceptably 'exceptional', this can leave wounds that never fully heal.

4

Young, Gifted and Black

'To be young, gifted and black,
Oh what a lovely precious dream
To be young, gifted and black,
Open your heart to what I mean
In the whole world you know
There are billion boys and girls
Who are young, gifted and black,
And that's a fact!'

WELDON IRVINE

Hosting *Live at the Apollo* in 2016, Gina Yashere tells the audience about breaking the news to her parents that she wanted to become a comedian. 'African family,' she declares, 'you've got four choices of career: doctor, lawyer, engineer ... disgrace to the family. My mum wasn't impressed when

I decided to become a comedian. She's like, "Comedy? Comedy? What the hell is comedy? How am I going to tell my friends back home in Nigeria? My daughter is a clown!"'

The preoccupation with certain careers is by no means solely Nigerian, or even African for that matter, with the joke landing just as well for many members of the Asian diaspora. By the time 'Young, Gifted and Black' was covered by the Jamaican duo Bob and Marcia, and went on to become a surprise hit in the UK, my dad's youngest brother Nkenna was just turning five years old. Not long after that, he would discover that he was one of the 'billion boys and girls who, as the song attests, happened to be gifted. Unfortunately, however, his gifts did not lend themselves to the aforementioned professions.

'When did I first discover my passion for football?' my uncle repeats back to me. 'You know, I think you're just born with it. That sort of passion isn't discovered or learned. It was almost religious to me.' Even now, at fifty-five speaking about football animates him in a way that little, other than his love for his son, has the capacity to. The youngest of my father's siblings, his Igbo name, Nkenna, literally translates as 'belonging to the father'. As we discuss his fervour for football, the complicated emotions that trace across his face as he recollects the friction that his talent would cause between himself and my grandfather are impossible to mask. 'I was to become a doctor or a lawyer, maybe an accountant, so that in the future I could provide for my family as a good father should.' Unlike the rest of his siblings, my uncle and his twin sister were born in London. This meant that whereas my dad and his older sister had early memories of the village, and had to adapt to the weight of expectations that came with the privileges of now being in Britain, my uncle had been shielded from the harsher realities of early years growing up in a war zone. His passion for extra-curricular activities outside of football, such as tennis and athletics, was fanned by my grandfather, who would regularly tune in to the tour events, Grand Slams and the Olympics. The football highlights, which hypnotised my uncle, would likewise leave my grandfather engrossed.

Despite growing up in Finsbury Park, within spitting distance of the old Highbury stadium, home of Arsenal Football Club, the player who drew my uncle's attention, much to the teasing of his friends and classmates, was Glenn Hoddle, who at the time played for local rivals Tottenham Hotspur. 'He just seemed to move differently. I loved watching him. He always had an extra second on the ball.' Did he ever see football players through the lens of race and think they were setting an example or blazing a trail for him to follow? 'Nah, I just loved good football and good players. Young enough, I could recognise I had a natural talent, so I just wanted to emulate the best.'

Unfortunately, my grandfather, sat alongside his youngest, saw the world of sport and football through less optimistic eyes. Long before the millionaire wages of the present day, the average wage of a football player in England's top division in 1975 was £116 a week, whereas an NHS GP would be earning more than £160. Equally concerning to my grandfather was the vile, openly racist language and taunts hurled at the handful of Black players who did manage to make it to play in the top flight, with monkey chants and banana skins regularly thrown onto the pitch. Clyde Best, one of the few Black players blazing a trail for the countless who would come after him, would later share one of the written threats he received that left him shaken: 'It warned me that as soon as I emerged from the tunnel and took to the field the following day, I would have acid thrown in my eyes,' Best recalled. This sport, which my uncle had fallen in love with, even though its supporters might not love him back, would become a major point of contention with my grandfather.

'I just couldn't make sense of it. He would encourage me on the one hand, like letting me play for school in local matches, but no further. When I was invited to trial for Islington? Nope. That got shut down. No explanation, just Dad's ruling. I had to focus on my school.' School, however, would bring its own complications.

With a large Irish Catholic and West Indian demographic in north London in the 1970s, the ethnic mix of the class-room was relatively diverse compared to other parts of the country at the time. Being one of the few Nigerian families who had recently moved to the area, however, was not unremarked upon. Factionalism, which still had lingering echoes when I was in the school playground, would run rife throughout my uncle's school years, as Black children wounded each other with barbs that hurt because of their ethnic specificity. It was not uncommon for my uncle to find himself racially abused on the street, be called 'nignog' or 'sambo' and have run-ins with white boys in the neighbourhood; however, his closest friends at school were white boys. The most contentious dynamic was between African and West Indian kids, tearing chunks out of each other verbally and sometimes literally in the school playground. Insults flew, as my family surname became 'YOU-WOO-GAH-LALA', while African kids would respond with jibes about knowing their true heritage, to which the reply would come that that was because their ancestors had sold fellow Black people into slavery. So it was that acts of love and familial affection would be subverted, teased and mocked.

Each fortnight, to ensure that my aunts' hair looked tidy and professional, my grandmother would plait it into neat corn rows. As each of the sisters grew older, they would plait each other's hair, a meticulous time-absorbing task infused with care. In the hands of those who knew the point of pride that hair took in Black families from any background, jibes about 'picky' hair that would snap the Afro-comb prongs because it was so tough and wire-like stung especially painfully. The fragrant home comforts of my grandmother's Nigerian cooking would linger on my uncle's school uniform, from which the accusation of him being a 'stinky African' did not follow far behind. Even as my uncle attempted to exercise his desire to, Dr Prentice-like, not see himself as defined by his race, the narratives of 'correct Blackness' would morph and modify with specific schoolyard taunts. As much as my grandparents spoke in their native tongue at home – and my uncle was surrounded by the trappings and Nigerian culture at home – he had not grown up in the village. Perhaps that's why my grand-father's extensive use of corporal punishment felt alien to him, even in the context of '70s Britain, where physically disciplining your child was not unheard of.

'It could be for anything: coming home late, failing a test, getting into a fight at school.' And there were fights. Where my father had nurtured an outlook of patience and tolerance, his younger brother was quicker to respond with action. 'I used to wonder, "Did they not get beats? Was it just me? Why does no one else in the family get in trouble?" But then I answered that for myself.' Even as my father managed to excel academically, his kid brother was struggling at school with 'could do better' and 'if only he applied him-self' – the consistent refrain from teachers at parent-teacher meetings and on report cards.

Now a father whose own son has been diagnosed with Attention Deficit Hyperactivity Disorder, he supposes that he was most likely undiagnosed as a child and is in the pro-cess of getting belatedly assessed himself. Unfortunately, ADHD would only be widely accepted as a valid condition in 2000, with the publication of the first National Institute of Clinical Excellence report on the condition, creating a deeper understanding about the wider societal effects of lack of awareness or misdiagnosis becoming more apparent as the condition is further researched. According to the charity ADHD Action, an estimated 30 per cent of adult prisoners have the condition. The compounding effects of a lack of understanding of the condition and high expectations from his parents and teachers, who perceived a disruptive child who didn't want to apply himself, resulted in fight after fight, row after row, 'when all I wanted to do, was play football. I was crazy about it.'

The saying goes that 'insanity is doing the same thing over and over and expecting a different result'. Perhaps my uncle was too stubborn for his own good, because despite my grandfather's best efforts, he could not be dissuaded. The drawback to living in such close proximity to his school meant there was no excuse for his late arrival home. However, the informal kickabouts that would happen in the schoolyard or park would prove too tempting a siren song to ignore. Each time the possibility to have the ball at his feet presented itself, the filial call to do as he was told and return home would become muted. Upon his return, the physical disciplining issued by my grandfather would follow as surely as my uncle would find himself back on the pitch at the very next opportunity. 'I remember specifically, it was the summer of '76. Obes, it was a scorcher. Every day during that summer holiday, I had to be out of the house, playing with the boys, kicking the ball around. I lived for it.'

As the years went by, frustrations grew and tensions increased: the unrelenting dreamer clashing with the indomitable will of his father. This tension would only be exacerbated when my uncle saw one of his white school-mates, Gary, get scouted to become part of the youth setup at a First Division club. His father had been involved with the local setup and, as such, football ran in the family. All throughout their school lives, Nkenna and Gary would be seen as the two exceptionally gifted local footballers. Gary would go on to play for several First Division teams, trav-elling up and down the country and plying his trade as a professional footballer. The influx of money that came with the Premier League and television rights just missed him, and he would change career in his later years, having not quite earned enough to see him comfortably into retirement. The pang that bumping into him causes my uncle is evi-dent in his eyes. 'You just wonder, you know? If I had done things differently, if Dad had supported me, even twenty per cent ... like, even twenty would have been enough, I'd have done the rest.' My grandfather, however, felt that he was left with no choice but to make the tough decision to support my uncle with more extreme measures, leading to a fracture in their relationship that proved difficult to mend.

The seemingly endless cycle that my uncle and grand-father were locked in showed very little sign of changing. The bull-headed determination to defy my grandfather and sneak out at every opportunity to play football went against not only my grandfather's hopes and ambitions for his youngest, but also the cultural and religious expec-tations of a son's deference to his father. 'I saw myself as a sinner. Growing up as we did, as Roman Catholics,

I felt like I was sinning by not doing as my father told me. Honour thy father and mother and all that. But I just couldn't help myself.'

Unfortunately, according to my uncle, it was my grandfather's misinformed ideas about the company his son kept and the negative impact they were having on him that would prove the proverbial straw that broke the camel's back. Despite the fact that all of his football-playing có-conspirators were white teenagers, my grandfather was convinced that he was 'hanging around with those Jamaican boys, running around being a criminal. Is that how you want to end up?' The racist narratives around young Black men and their criminality had reared its odious head and no amount of protesting would convince him otherwise. When he was barely into his teens, my uncle had his first few run-ins with the police, with early morning magistrate appearances breaking the hearts of my grandparents. Fearing for their son's safety if he fell by the wayside, they took the course of action taken by many parents of his generation and plenty more since.

My uncle was fourteen when he boarded the plane to Nigeria, accompanied by his twin sister and his parents. Although he hadn't grown up in Nigeria, the language and food had been in the house to the extent that it did not feel alien. 'I loved that side of things. The music, the food, the heat!' But for a young boy born in London, nothing could prepare him for what came next. Two weeks into their stay in my grandmother's village, he woke up and went to look for his sister and parents. Asking one of his distant uncles of their whereabouts, he was met with, 'Ah! They've gone back to London now. You go stay here oh.'

'I was in shock, Obes. Stay here? Without Twin? Without my brother and sisters? Mum and Dad. I just ...' He trailed off.

The Igbo saying *'Oha n a azu nwa'* has various permutations around the continent, but the meaning that it captures is the same: 'It takes a village to raise a child.' In many African cultures this is meant in a literal sense. If you're caught acting out of line by any of your elders, be they distant cousins, friends of the family or even neighbours, they would feel they were within their rights to reprimand and even physically discipline you. My grandfather, despairing at the stubbornness of his youngest son, and deprived of the extended familial structures he had grown up around, believed that the best thing for this errant teenage boy was the strictness and discipline of back home; the familial rod of correction.

'I still believe to this day, Obi,' my uncle says, fixing my gaze, 'if they had known what would happen to me during those years, they would have been on a flight the next day to bring me home.' My grandparents, however, believed they were doing the best they could for their youngest and, with what money they had, had enrolled him at the boarding school near to where the rest of my family came from in the east of Nigeria, deprived of any other options.

*

Nigeria's connection to Britain far predates my grandparents' journey to the country. It is estimated that 1.4 million Igbo people were captured, enslaved and transported across the Atlantic, in the main by British ships. Between 1650 and 1900, approximately one out of every eight slaves was taken from the Bight of Biafra in what would go on to be called the Southern Nigerian Protectorate. The impact of the British Empire would go far beyond just the slave trade that destroyed families and robbed generations of men and women of all ages. Although it is often applauded as forward thinking, in being one of the first countries to abolish the slave trade (though Haiti was the first), Britain's motives were not primarily benevolent. Upon analysing the cost-effectiveness of maintaining the slave trade compared to the profits made from Caribbean sugar imports, Britain slowly phased out the buying and selling of human beings.

Many historians have praised Britain's West Africa Squadron for capturing some 1,600 slave ships and freeing 150,000 enslaved Africans, while somehow glossing over the fact that it was the slave owners in Jamaica, not the emancipated slaves, who were compensated to the tune of £20,000,000 in reparations after the eradication of the vile practice. The commitment that the British government undertook would keep them indebted to former slave owners until 2015.

The British policy towards Nigeria changed from one of aggressive domination to a more supervisory role, using local emirs in the largely Muslim north of the country as 'native authorities', and interacting with local village chiefs in the south through indirect rule to ensure their authority. One of the side effects of the north of the country being majority Muslim was that the missionaries who came to the country were advised not to evangelise in that region. Lord Lugard, British governor of Nigeria from 1914 to 1919, was a fan of the Hausa-Fulani hierarchical social structure in northern Nigeria, referring to them as more developed than the 'tribes' of the south. This is largely why the majority of missionary schools, established as a means of civilising the local populations, were initially located in the coastal regions and then, later, further inland.

Inherent in Western teaching at these missionary schools, however, were colonial attitudes to both gender and discipline. Not only was it some years before girls were permitted access to these schools, but British administrators encouraged the promotion of male chiefs as their primary points of contact, entrenching notions of gender inequality that would be internalised in the years to come. Though there is little literature on the subject, what there is maintains that beatings and corporal punishments were not as common in sub-Saharan Africa prior to the colonial period. While physical discipline did happen, it was undertaken by family members or as part of a larger initiation ceremony. With the mission schools, and later the state-run schools, the notion of physical disciplining, particularly flogging, became more commonplace: 'legitimacy accrued to beating primarily by virtue of it being a particularly European practice', as the historian Steven Pierce described it. Teachers, friends of the family and neighbours felt it was their duty to keep children in line. Perversely, it would be this mentality that would go on to be internalised by Nigerians after colonisation as somehow inherently African, or a cultural norm, and be maintained throughout the diaspora.

In impossible situations, impossible choices were made. Unfortunately, the dynamic between my grandfather and his youngest son was not an anomaly, with the story repeating across communities as Black parents tried to negotiate how best they might be able to protect their children against the daunting world over which they had no control and which was not designed to support them. Despairing at losing his son to the care system, and fully aware that police use of the 'sus law'* was being used disproportionately against Black men and women, my grandfather felt there was no other option. The sacrifice my grandparents had made, coupled with their awareness of their privilege in being able to resettle in London, meant that the idea of losing their youngest son to the justice system was unfathomable. For my uncle, his sense of abandonment and his parents' lack of faith in his ability to reform was catastrophic.

'I blocked out most of it, if I'm honest, Obes. The trauma of it was a lot. Beats was one thing . . . and there were beats. From teachers to uncles to people I didn't even know. School

* A stop and search law created under the 1824 Vagrancy Act that gave police officers the power to arrest anyone they suspected of loitering with the intent to commit a crime.

didn't get any easier over there; just more strict. But, beyond that, I just thought, you know what? I'll show you. If that's all you think I can be, Dad, then maybe that's all I am.'

It would be the best part of three years before my uncle returned to London, yet the fissure between father and son would only continue to deepen, with my uncle deciding to neither take up football nor fully return to the academic path his father wanted for him as a form of security. He lasted one month on an engineering apprenticeship, before looking elsewhere for employment.

Now that he is a grown man and a father himself, what lessons does he think he's learned about being a Black man? 'It's funny now I'm older, but I do believe your granddad was right. I say to my son, "You know, education is the greatest gift that I can give you. It opens up so many doors." He was right about that.' Knowing all of that, does he think he would have been happy going down the football route, even though he would have only played for a maximum of twenty years? He almost interrupts me, he's so certain. 'Absolutely. Absolutely. Twenty years of playing in front of crowds, setting up goals, scoring goals. I would have been happy. I don't think you can place a price on that. Just living a happy life. Not exceptional, just happy.'

My own fascination with being an actor began with my eldest brother. Surrounded as I was by positive role models, both friends and family, he was what I first thought of as 'cool'. My parents, with three boys each three years apart, were loath to give away clothes to charity shops if one of the younger siblings could fit into them, and I was an ever eager recipient of the sartorial choices of my older brothers. Watching my eldest brother's early rugby matches from the sidelines, I set my sights on becoming the rugby 1st XV captain. Hearing that he was playing for the county team, it seemed not only a trail that had been blazed but an inevitability that I had to follow. Our school was entirely single-sex apart from the sixth form, which allowed in a small cohort of girls from both neighbouring and more distant schools. Commenting on his choices for extra-curricular activities, he gave a winning smile as he said, 'You've gotta do drama, man. That's what all the girls do. And they're buff too!' I was only eleven years old, but took much of what my brother said as gospel. And yet, when I pilfered his A-level text of the paired Arthur Miller plays 'A View from the Bridge/All My Sons', I was transported. Devouring both plays in one sitting, my appetite was voracious. It wasn't long before I'd tracked down his complete works in the local library and, like a series drop on Netflix, inhaled each of his offerings.

Before long it was Tennessee Williams, then Eugene O'Neill, Chekhov to Ibsen and Noël Coward to Neil Simon. When my library didn't have the offering that I was after, and without the disposable cash to buy it myself, I would read as many scenes as I could in Foyles on Charing Cross Road before a shop assistant realised that I was not so much browsing as getting my theatrical fix, as I hunched on a stool far too small for me. My parents supported me: 'As long as you keep up in school, and if you're gonna do something, DO it. Half-hearted is no way to do anything in life.' As much as I enjoyed the piano, I found practising it a chore. It was a point of contention between me and my parents, who would insist that I upheld my end of the bargain by properly preparing for the lessons they were providing.

Knowing my susceptibility to a good story, my father would go on to paraphrase one of our oft-watched family films, *The Karate Kid*, as a way to illustrate his point. 'In life, don't bother with guess so.' He would say, 'It's not worth it. Just like Mr Miyagi says to Daniel-san, "Karate yes" or "Karate no"? Great. "Karate maybe?" You'll just get carried away on the whims of other people.' Not long after, I would quit my piano lessons. Acting and singing, however, felt like where I came alive and what I needed to do. So, for seven years, my Saturday schedule consisted of making my way across London to get on a coach to a rugby away game at some private school in the home counties, then making my way back across London to the Anna Scher Theatre for a two-hour drama class that cost a fiver, before one last journey back to south-west London, where I would rehearse and sing High Mass at the Brompton Oratory from 5 until 7 p.m. By the time I returned home to Holloway, I felt both sated and invigorated. My love of storytelling had been released, Pandora-like, and there was little hope of me cramming the desire to be an actor back into the box.

Perhaps it was the knowledge that my father was so exceptional which filled me with trepidation; that he would place pressure on me to be or make certain career choices to be like him, and I was unsure if I would be a disappointment to him. Or perhaps it was the fear of him disappointing me. In my head I ran through the confrontation that was sure to come, and my many-reasoned defences. Contrary to our preliminary conversations, I had decided that I wouldn't be taking Biology and Chemistry A levels as they didn't fit in with music and drama in the scheduling. I'd decided that I really did want to be an actor; that was the best thing for me, and the thing that would make me happy and that I would make it work. I hoped he understood. Dad, as ever, would surprise me.

'Okay, son, sounds good.'

I felt the sensation of a door swinging open when it gives nowhere near the resistance you expect. Stumbling through, I tried to regain my composure, attempting to contextualise my surprise at his acceptance of my academic choices. 'So, you're okay with me not doing any sciences for A level?'

'Obi, all your mum and I want and have ever wanted is for you to be happy. The only person who you will live with for the rest of your life and must justify all your decisions to is you.'

'I dunno. I guess I always thought you wanted me to be a doctor,' I mumbled, realising that those words had never left either of my parents' mouths. I felt both foolish and relieved, and still in need of reassurance. I pushed my luck. 'But I thought you'd want me to do something safer and more secure, that the world might see me differently.'

'They will. But you can't let that hold you back. I know that I have been over-qualified for jobs they wouldn't offer me for whatever reason. I have had appraisals where there has been no reason for them to not promote me. It cannot be where you decide who you are. If it is, you will lose. Every time you lose your temper at a teacher or lash out at a boss, you reaffirm their image of you. Even when you succeed, which God willing you will, it will never be enough for them.'

I have been blessed in many ways in the home I grew up in, not least in the amount of physical affection that both my parents felt comfortable giving me. My need for a hug in that moment was as much a recognition of the validation my father had given me as it was an expression of feeling safe in the freedom of who or what I could be in the arms of one of the biggest influences in my life. My father didn't need to say who the 'them' was he was referring to. I would see it all around me. 'To be young, gifted and Black' was indeed a precious dream. However, I felt in my father's hug an acknowledgement of the frailty of that dream. Unlike Dr Prentice, my father was all too aware that he was a 'coloured man', and he navigated the world fully cognisant of it. His leonine protectiveness of my own dreams was reminiscent of Richard Williams, father of two of my idols, Venus and Serena Williams.

During an interview for ABC News, back in 1995, the fourteen-year-old tennis prodigy Venus is quizzed on her confidence in her ability to beat her unnamed opponent.

When she replies that she is indeed 'very confident', the male interviewer then begins to ask her about the reason she's so sure of her abilities: 'You say it so easily. Why?' Having heard enough, her father Richard interjects. 'What she said, she said it with so much confidence the first time, but you keep going on and on,' he said. 'You've got to understand that you're dealing with the image of a fourteen-year-old child. And this child gonna be out there playing when you're old. You and me gonna be in the grave. When she say something, we done told you what's happening. You're dealing with a little Black kid, and let her be a kid! She done answered it with a lot of confidence, leave that alone!'

My father, just like Richard, was more than aware that his sons would be held to a different standard in much the same way that he had been. So, even as he dared me to dream and be active in chasing whatever made me completely happy, he balanced that with a sharp reminder that the world was indeed unfair, urging me to eschew 'guess so' listlessness. I would have to do what made me happy, in spite of the white gaze around me and sometimes because of it. If I was aiming to gain admission to a club that, consciously or not, did not want me to be a member, I would be sorely let down not only by my own misplaced hope but also by friends and colleagues who watched blatant injustices occur and did not speak up. He had seen that 'Black excellence' did little to insulate him or the Black men he saw in the world around him.

*

When, in 2018, the Gabonese striker Pierre-Emerick Aubameyang had a banana skin hurled at him while playing for Arsenal in the north London derby, the incident was met with shock and disbelief by commentators who believed that the days of racist football fans had been left in some distant, far less civilised past. Britain, they told themselves, was beyond racism, and the evidence of that was in more than 30 per cent of professional football players being Black. Only a year prior to this, the journalist Brendan O'Neill opined that, 'The truth is that racism has disappeared from the game. There is nothing like the racial tensions of a few decades ago. Kids of every colour worship Black players.' Our memories, however, can play tricks on us, and perhaps it slipped O'Neill's mind that former England captain Rio Ferdinand had seen his international career wrecked after John Terry was accused of racially abusing Rio's younger brother Anton in 2011, allegedly calling him a 'fucking Black cunt'. While Terry was acquitted at the criminal trial, an independent FA tribunal found enough evidence to punish Terry with a four-game ban and a £220,000 fine. Although the older Ferdinand had a wealth of international experience, the England manager at the time, Roy Hodgson, opted not to select him for the upcoming international game where he would have to play alongside Terry due to 'footballing reasons'. Those who found the rationale behind the decision patchy at best had their credulity stretched when, after an injury forced Gary Cahill to withdraw from the fixture, Hodgson chose to call up twenty-two-year-old Martin

Kelly, with two minutes of international experience, rather than the eighty-two-times capped Ferdinand. Writing about the incident years later, Ferdinand pointed to the strain it put on his family.

'My brother Anton, the innocent party in all this, had his career damaged and was subjected to death threats. There were bullets in the post, and unending racist abuse ... My mum had her windows smashed and bullets put through her door, and ended up in hospital with a virus because of the stress.'

As with many Black men who had seen their career hit unexpected speed bumps or roadblocks, Ferdinand was given what he felt were unsatisfactory answers as to why his career had lost momentum, with race the unfortunate elephant in the room. The incident would also go on to ruin one of Ferdinand's longest friendships with fellow England defender Ashley Cole. Texting just before the trial, Ferdinand left him with an ultimatum.

'I told him he had a choice: "You're my mate and you're John Terry's mate. You know both our families. So go into court and tell the exact truth about what happened, or don't go at all." He told me, "I've got no choice, I've been told I've got to go." I said, "Well, if you do go just know this: we will never talk again. You know what happened. You saw it."'

With race looming so large in the conversation, Ashley's defence of Terry placed him in a lose-lose situation, which neither he nor Ferdinand had instigated. With such flimsy reasons given for dropping Ferdinand, Cole must have been keenly aware that, despite being one of the few indisputably world-class players in the team, his name on the team sheet was not a certainty. Either he could stand shoulder to shoulder with Terry, providing him with a supporting statement and risk fracturing his long-standing friendship with Ferdinand, or state publicly that his club and international teammate had been racially abusive and make himself a target for the kind of racist abuse that Rio had opened himself up to by standing by his brother.

From Ferdinand's point of view, when Cole made the perhaps understandable, if frustratingly pragmatic, choice of protecting his club teammate and his reputation, he was choosing personal allegiances over the perceived larger crime of a racist attack. Ferdinand's ire was such that he re-tweeted a comment on Twitter, referring to Cole as a 'choc-ice', comparable to a 'Bounty' by being Black on the outside and white on the inside, which would land him with a fine of £45,000 from the FA.

Britain's complicated and unexamined relationship with race was yet again rearing its head in the most unlikely of scenarios. Despite both being professionals at the top of their game, neither of whom had been directly involved in the incident, it threatened to derail both their careers and led to vitriol emanating wildly in a sport that supposedly 'had no issue with race'. The despair felt by Black players who had done well enough to be worshipped 'by kids of every colour', only to then be subjected to monkey chants and banana skins being hurled at them, can only have been made worse by the feeble punishments that the footballing authorities dished out for such behaviour. It is no wonder that certain players, such as Tottenham and England's Danny Rose, would make headlines stating, 'I've had enough. How I programme myself is that I think I've got five or six more years left in football, and I just can't wait to see the back of it.'

His comments came fresh from the racist abuse that he, Callum Hudson-Odoi and Raheem Sterling were subjected to in the England match against Montenegro in March 2019. One becomes more sympathetic to Rose's comments when confronted with the fact that UEFA fined the Montenegro FA 20,000 Euros for racial abuse that could be heard even in the television broadcast.

The priorities of the authorities in charge of protecting footballers from racist abuse, as is their duty, are clear. When in 2012, Nicklas Bendtner displayed his underwear, which featured the Paddy Power logo as part of his goal celebration, UEFA handed him an £80,000 fine. Despite being elite-level athletes – the literal definition of Black excellence both at home and abroad – Black players are consistently subjected to racist abuse and are supposed to be happy to accept the paltry defence that it's 'nothing like the racial tension of decades ago'. And the blind spot extends beyond individual journalists.

The English FA, in its report about racist comments made in 2014 by the then England Women's coach, Mark Sampson, to Eniola Aluko concluded, despite finding that Sampson had made remarks that were 'discriminatory on the grounds of race', that they did not believe he was racist. The broader, insidious and at times unconscious nature of racist acts, however, does not mean that they are any less strongly felt by Black people. The effects of this are as widespread as they are deleterious.

In 2020, a Danish research firm carried out a study aimed at understanding whether the football media talks differently about players depending on their skin tone. More than 2,000 statements from commentary on eighty games across the Premier League, Serie A, La Liga and Ligue 1 were analysed. It found that commentators are more than six times more likely to talk about the power of a player if he has darker skin and three times more likely to reference his pace. In isolation, of course, these statements feel innocuous. However, when coupled with racist stereotypes, the impact is marked. If Black players are seen as naturally physically gifted rather than being possessed of the intelligence or creativity that their white counterparts are praised for, is it any wonder that, as their body gives up on them, despite making up nearly a third of all professional footballers in England, only six of the ninety-two head coaches in England's professional leagues are Black or non-white? The direct link between how Black players are portrayed in the media and the racist abuse they receive was directly called out by Raheem Sterling, after he was racially abused during a game between Manchester City and Chelsea in 2018. The forward would write on his social media accounts:

'Regarding what was said at the Chelsea game, as you can see by my reaction I just had to laugh because I don't expect no better.' At only twenty-four years of age, Sterling had already formed defence mechanisms for the racist treatment he consistently receives.

His point, however, extended far beyond his own personal experience. Posting two articles published in the same year, Sterling highlighted the stark difference in language choice used to discuss teammates Tosin Adarabioyo and Phil Foden. Foden was praised in glowing terms as a 'starlet' for buying his mother a £2m home, whereas British-Nigerian Adarabioyo, who similarly bought his mother a house on the market for £2.25m, was framed as 'having never started a Premier League match'. Raheem continued, 'For all the newspapers that don't understand why people are racist in this day and age, all I have to say is have a second thought about fair publicity and give all players an equal chance.'

Ultimately, all Sterling is asking for is equal treatment but, as a young Black man, he knows all too well that this will not be forthcoming. Sadly, he is aware that the structures in place to protect him as a footballer are often more concerned with exploiting his talent rather than enacting the necessary work to ensure he has a safe working environment.

Raheem Sterling has come under intense media scrutiny throughout his career despite, or perhaps because of, consistently playing himself into contention to be the league's top scorer. He has alternatively been portrayed as miserly, due to flying with budget airlines or shopping at Poundland; flashy, when *The Sun* worked out the total cost of each car Raheem had ever driven, and he was even linked to gun violence after getting a tattoo in honour of his father who was tragically shot. The criticism levelled at him would be laughable were it not so targeted and malicious. This unfounded targeting of the player reached a particularly intense frenzy in the run-up to the Euro 2016 competition. Feeling overwhelmed, he confided in one of his coaches at the time, Gary Neville:

'As a coach, on reflection, I didn't really know how to deal with it and I went into a protective mode and thought about how I would get one of our most important players ready for the next match. I told him he was a great player and we loved him to bits, which we did – he played nearly all the games for us – and tried to almost patch him up to get him to a point where he can play without addressing the underlying issue. But, on reflection now, that may have been brushing it aside a little bit, in all honesty. I told him he was strong and good enough to play for England and that it had happened to players before him. But there was a deep-down understanding that there was a total differ-ence to the attacks he was getting compared to others. He was and is willing to stand up and carry on playing to an outstanding level, but he's been carrying this now for years; this is not just a Chelsea fan at the weekend, it's been going on for years with him. It's a really difficult situation and one which I think, "How I would deal with it if he is put

in that situation again? How would I try and help him?"
He's a tough lad to come through everything he's come
through, and the scrutiny, to perform like he has done, is
a miracle almost.'

Credit must go to Neville and the level of introspection
he employed in recognising how he might have done better
in that situation. Unfortunately, racism is a hydra whose
roots have seeped deep into the fabric of so many aspects
of our lives. Presented with the predicament of one Black
player – and knowing that the treatment he has been receiving from the media is different to white players past and
present, from David Beckham to Harry Kane – much like
a trainer in a boxing match, he opted to patch him up and
try to have him fighting fit rather than grapple with a meg-
alith that has a history centuries long. Neville recognised
the 'difficult situation' Sterling, at a mere twenty-two years
of age, was in. He acknowledged the targeted nature of the
attacks, but he was relying on the resilience of this young
man to, Atlas-like, bear the weight of that situation on his
shoulders. What was most important was not the chastising
of the national press, but for Sterling to be confident enough
in his own ability to 'prove the critics wrong'. Recognising
the undue scrutiny and pressure he has been put through,
he valorises Sterling and his ability to succeed despite the
odds (a 'miracle almost'). The pastoral care that Sterling
might be afforded in addressing the problem in his workplace, however, was noticeably absent. Is it fair to expect
one coach or indeed one player to singlehandedly challenge

racist stereotypes of Black athletes? And yet, even while acknowledging the unfair treatment that Sterling receives, and showing support for the player, he is still limited by what is deemed 'acceptable' for a Black athlete.

During the same edition of *Monday Night Football* where Neville recalled his interaction with Sterling, Jamie Carragher thought back on his own time playing alongside Sterling. In seeking to defend him, he asked: 'What is the perception of Raheem Sterling in this country for most people, who buy papers and read media stuff online?' He went on to answer his own question. 'The perception is of a young, flashy Black kid from London, really, and a lot of it comes from the fact that maybe he moved on from Liverpool ... the perception that he's more interested in cars, jewellery and nightclubs rather than his actual football. Anyone reading that, anyone writing that, I can assure you that is absolute, utter nonsense. It's garbage. Raheem Sterling's a mouse.'

Even within his attempt to speak out on behalf of the player, Carragher found himself adopting the media line that somehow his being a 'young, flashy Black kid from London' is inherently wrong. The standards by which he was being held were so patently different to the countless other Premier League stars who were millionaires and have every right to use their wealth however they so feel. The danger of such a defence is that it cements the notion that there is in fact a *right* way to be a Black man. That if Sterling had just been humble enough, or flashier, or had not shopped in the pound saver store or had not demanded a pay rise or had driven a humble Fiat rather than a sports car, that he may *somehow* have evaded the ire and vitriol of the press.

What Carragher perhaps failed to take into account is that the journalists who ran the headlines such as 'Life and times of footie idiot Raheem Sterling', where they criticised him for showing off the house he had bought, were more interested in castigating him than they were the newsworthiness of any such story. As praiseworthy as Sterling's resilience in the face of undue targeting was – coupled with his being one of the few people brave enough to call out the media's unfair treatment – it is not a burden that he should have to bear. That burden represents a worrying trend in how Black men are treated.

The canonisation that certain Black men are granted is not accidental. By the time Martin Luther King Jr was assassinated, he had been called 'the most dangerous man in America' by the FBI, who had a 17,000-page file on him. During his lifetime, he was considered a radical demagogue, with many congressmen believing his 1963 March on Washington where he would make his infamous 'I Have a Dream' speech, to be potentially seditious. Just before the March on Washington, a Gallup survey found that only 23 per cent of Americans had favourable opinions of the proposed civil rights demonstration. After his death, however, it became easier to forget that he was considered a dangerous revolutionary who was both anti-imperialist and anti-capitalist. He would become posthumously used as a rod to chastise those who might pick up his baton in the struggle for civil rights. Quotes taken out of context would be appropriated by politicians such as Ronald Reagan to critique affirmative action for under-served Americans. Others, such as former Republican presidential candidate Mike Huckabee, would in 2015 claim to know what Dr King would have thought about the Black Lives Matter movement. 'When I hear people scream, "Black Lives Matter!" I think, of course they do ... But all lives matter. It's not that any life matters more than another.'

During the 2016 NFL season, more than fifty years after Dr King's March on Washington, 49ers quarterback Colin Kaepernick attracted nationwide attention with his decision to kneel during the playing of 'The Star-Spangled Banner'. Initially, Kaepernick had been moved to sit during the national anthem as a form of protest in the aftermath of the police shootings of Alton Sterling and Philando Castile. Kaepernick would go on to explain his decision not to stand, stating, 'I am not going to stand up to show pride in a flag for a country that oppresses Black people and People of Color. To me, this is bigger than football and it would be selfish on my part to look the other way. There are bodies in the street and people getting paid leave and getting away with murder.'

However, Nate Boyer, a former NFL player and army veteran, advised Kaepernick to take a knee instead of sitting down, stating, 'In my opinions and in my experience, kneeling's never been in our history really seen as a disrespectful act. I mean, people kneel when they get knighted. You kneel to propose to your wife, and you take a knee to pray. And soldiers often take a knee in front of a fallen brother's grave to pay respects. So I thought, if anything, besides standing, that was the most respectful.'

Before long, the protest would be seen as a symbol of solidarity for the mistreatment of Black citizens by their government, not just in the US but globally. Despite the attempt to respectfully protest, the symbol would be roundly criticised in many quarters, however, with perhaps the most public criticism coming from President Trump. Speaking at one of his rallies in 2017, he challenged NFL commissioners on the protests, stating, 'Wouldn't you love to see one of these NFL owners, when somebody disrespects our flag, to say, "Get that son of a bitch off the field right now. Out! He's fired. He's fired!"'

Back in Britain, Foreign Secretary Dominic Raab would be roundly mocked when attempting to assert that he believed the origins of taking the knee had its genesis in *Game of Thrones*. The patent insincerity of that statement was thrown into sharp relief when he proudly boasted seconds later that he would only 'take the knee for two people: the Queen and the missus when I asked her to marry me.' The failure of the Foreign Secretary to be better versed on an action that would become synonymous with a global movement is compounded by the very real damage that engaging in off-the-cuff frippery causes. Consciously or not, the trivialising of Black peoples' concerns about the systemic layers of oppression they feel in all walks of life, and for which they demand redress, is not befitting of a cabinet minister. Later in the interview, Raab would go on to implicitly criticise Black people for employing a gesture he described as 'a symbol of subjugation and subordination rather than one of liberation and emancipation'. The fact that as a society we are more uncomfortable with the manner in which people protest than the deep injustice they are protesting speaks volumes. Or as activist and actor Jesse Williams phrased it: 'If you have a critique for the resistance, for our resistance, then you better have an established record of critique of our oppression.'

Dr King has been celebrated since his death for his profound commitment to nonviolence, calling it a 'powerful and just weapon which cuts without wounding and ennobles the man who wields it'. His saintly ability to peacefully demand change in the face of violence is seen by many as the method that those who have come after him should emulate. The sanitised children's books that I would read about Dr King emphasised his biography as a Christian preacher and man of God who preached the philosophy of 'turning the other cheek' and loving your enemies.

In an interview with Sophie Ridge in 2020, Conservative Party Chairman James Cleverly asserted that in his opinion Britain was 'one of the least racist, one of the most open and welcoming countries in the world', pointing to surveys about how national and global attitudes had shifted over the past few decades. For those British people, however, who are victims of racism, statements like Cleverly's read as if Black people should feel grateful that their cup of wine is only a tenth mixed with cyanide, because previously it was half and half. It should not be unreasonable for a citizen to demand that their government does everything in its power to protect them from the insidious effects of discrimination.

Cleverly's desire seems to be for Black people to love their so-called 'enemies' due to the perceived progress that has been made, rather than demanding that those in charge strive for greater progress and further strides towards equality. The danger of extolling these certain virtues of Dr King and setting them up as the paradigm to be followed by those seeking to effect change, however, is that it places the onus on the victim to change the mind of their oppressor. In asking somebody who has been struck in the face to turn the other cheek rather than critiquing the attacker for striking the victim, there is a degree of victim-blaming at play. In Stokely Carmichael's damning indictment of Dr King's methods of nonviolence, the prominent civil rights activist stated, 'In order for nonviolence to work, your opponent must have a conscience. The United States has none.'

The insidious nature of racism and sexism is exacerbated by a reluctance on the part of the individual to accept that passivity or ignorance to larger societal issues allows them to be maintained on a wider, societal level. Carmichael's words rankle because they paint so many in the role of the oppressor. We have come to learn that racism and sexism are negative attributes, but the majority self-identify as good people with consciences; therefore we do not consciously participate in oppressive behaviours. This leaves us in a racist and sexist world supposedly without any racists or sexists. Perhaps this is one of the reasons why the methods of Dr King are held up as the ideal form of protest; because they require no work from the greater whole. It does not require individual people to unlearn any internalised notions around race or gender.

Whether *meant* maliciously or not, everyday Black women and men must tolerate comments about their Afro hair being unprofessional, embarrassing bastardisations of their names, and more than nine out of ten Black children report hearing racist language at school, and almost half believe it to be their biggest barrier to success. If a customer, upon entering a vase shop, accidentally breaks a vase, the shop owner might forgive them and ask them to be more aware and careful in future. If, however, the customer continues to walk around the shop and breaks vases every thirty seconds or so, the shop owner would be forgiven for believing it was intentional. Ultimately, whatever the customer's intentions or protestations of innocence, the damage is done and, once the customer has left without buying anything, the owner is left picking up the pieces without having even sold a vase. In framing racism and sexism as matters of active or wilful acts or prejudice, it blinds us to the damage and harm we reck-lessly effect and stifles the opportunity for self-correction.

It was also why some members of the Black community were dubious about the media's motives in reporting the story of Patrick Hutchinson at the London Black Lives Matter counter-protests in the summer of 2020. Far-right activists from around the country had travelled to the capital to protest against Black Lives Matter groups. Hundreds of protestors clashed with police, injuring officers as punches, kicks and missiles were thrown by demonstrators who claimed to be protecting statues. Hutchinson, along with four of his friends, decided to attend the protest to 'try to keep the peace'. As one white counter-protestor, former police officer Bryn Male, became isolated from his group, witnesses reported someone saying, 'Fuck Black Lives Matter.' He was subsequently surrounded by and assaulted by a group of young protestors of all races. Sensing that Male's life was in danger, Hutchinson lifted the man onto his shoulders and carried him to the safety of the police. The image of the white counter-protestor being carried out of danger on the shoulders of the Black grandfather quickly went viral with politicians celebrating Hutchinson as 'a national hero'. The media's desire to latch onto the feel-good story of a Black man who did the right thing, despite ideological differences, is understandable, but once more reinforces the notion that the cure to racism lies on the literal and figurative shoulders of Black men and women.

Lee Russell was one of the men who helped form a protective ring so that Male could be lifted to safety. He would reveal after the fact: 'My thing was not really saving that man. It was more saving one of these Black kids that was attacking that guy – their life could be gone, as well as the gentleman's. A wasted life in prison because of those moments of madness.'

For many parents, one of the earliest and sometimes dreaded conversations is started when a child asks, 'Where do babies come from?' Euphemisms abound as age-appropriate, if frustratingly heteronormative, allegories about 'the birds and the bees' and 'when a man and a woman love each other very much' are employed to talk about the joy of new life. However, the collective responsibility that Black people in this country have historically felt in navigating racism in Britain is often distilled into a different conversation: 'The Talk'. There is a near-universal moment of discomfiture when as a parent of a Black child you must have a discussion where you reveal that because of the colour of their skin, they will be treated differently. More often than not it is a series of conversations where a parent attempts to equip their child with tools that might serve to protect them from some of the racist interactions they might experience.

In the summer of 2020, several prominent Black Britons shared their own experiences of said conversations in the Channel 4 programme *The Talk*. The journalist Gary Younge would recount his father telling him: 'Racism is not your fault, but it's going to be your challenge and your responsibility to find your way through it so that you can live the life that you want to live.' Immediately as I started watching the show I felt a deep unease creeping over me. The familiarity of so many of the conversations, from broadcasters and choreographers to performers like Emeli Sandé or actor Lennie James, unsettled me; the universality of the experiences and the methods of protection disturbing. Newscaster Gillian Joseph distilled it simply: 'We have to prepare our children. We are forced to prepare our children.'

As my disquiet grew, I tried to ascertain why this programme was affecting me so much. Sandé went on to share a story from her childhood. When she was four years old and had her face painted at a school fair, an older lady came over to her and proclaimed, 'I didn't know butterflies could be brown.' It emerged as a slow dawning. One by one, I was witnessing Black people from all walks of life detailing and recounting traumatic experiences that had happened in their life. I recognised the protective parental fury of an adult confronting her child with an unwarranted racist statement when she had barely left nursery. Or Tinie Tempah's father declaring that the 'best way to win a fight was to avoid it'. I sat uncomfortably as singer and presenter Rochelle Humes shared being barred from attending a friend's party because her friend's father had said, 'You can't come to the party because you're Black.' Struggling to hold back tears, she would ruminate on scrubbing her legs raw in the bath as she tried to scrub her skin off.

But before long, my discomfort grew to a frustration. None of these stories felt outlandish or impossible to me, nor could I imagine that they felt alien to many other Black viewers. But once more, that recurring motif of personal responsibility had resurfaced – how a Black child might navigate the currents and storms of the underlying racism within Britain. As each contributor recalled past trauma, I questioned the point of the programme. For whom are they reliving this trauma? Many Black viewers already knew and empathised with the experiences they were hearing, so it wasn't new or novel to the majority of them. Was it then for the majority of white viewers? Perhaps. There is a distinct power in testimony and personal lived experience, especially from those who are in the public eye. Perhaps a percentage of the viewers suddenly had their eyes opened to the travesties that many Black people have had to face in Britain and the double standards they have been subjected to. I began to realise my frustration lay in who was expected to have 'The Talk' and who was deemed 'too innocent' to discuss the blight of racism on our society.

At the age of four, Emeli Sandé was old enough to experience racial abuse from an adult, and yet she would have to be taught about how society would see her. At the age of eleven, accosted by a police officer, Lennie James would be told to 'shut his N-word mouth', but it was he who would have to learn how to navigate racism. In the face of the momentum of waves of individual racist comments and wider narratives that have been taught about Black people in this country, how many viewers who were not Black would be sitting down to have 'The Talk' with their children? Or did they believe that witnessing the testimony would be enough? Perhaps, that Black people by virtue of being patient, turning the other cheek and being the 'right kind of Black person' might overcome racism. My frustration with the show would pique at its denouement, when Marvin Humes, husband to Rochelle and father of their daughter, said: 'Our seven-year-old has started to ask questions. She's seen the Black Lives Matter protests on the TV. When is the right time to have that conversation with her, if we even have to have that conversation because she's so innocent? She's not come across racism, yet, to her personally.' Rochelle's reply, however, would give me hope. 'I just don't want her to not be armed with the right information.'

It is a place of privilege to be able to not discuss larger issues in society, such as racism and sexism merely because they may not affect us personally. Humes's daughter is the same age as she was when a classmate parroted racist comments that she had learned from her father. Unfortunately, the changing of the tide *is* a matter of personal responsibility. We are all personally responsible for the wider narratives that we choose to teach, listen to and internalise. The ability to succeed in society should not be dependent on Black people's ability to fit into a narrowed view of what is acceptable purely because of racist narratives around Blackness. Perhaps if Gary Neville had had some of those same conversations when he was younger, he might have felt better equipped to support one of his charges when dealing with the issue of racism in the media rather than 'brushing it aside' and relying on Sterling's almost miraculous resilience to pull through.

The awkwardness around talking about race is often cloaked in language around innocence lost or the complexity of the conversation. However, many parents would willingly enter into conversations about love, empathy and forgiveness, which I can attest from personal experience are complex ideas that many grown adults are still grappling with. Ignorance can no longer be a defence. Once we know more, we must do more. The harsh reality is that the longer non-Black parents shy away from these awkward conversations, the longer we delay moving towards a fairer and more just society. Regrettably, the appetite for Black people to shoulder the burden of racism and manufacture its solution fosters an environment where police officers, journalists or sports fans feel no incentive to challenge the ideas they have about Black people.

Relying on 'Black excellence' as a defence against racism has its limitations, as Patrick Hutchinson would learn. Despite rescuing Bryn Male from impeding danger and extricating him from a situation in which he was being physically assaulted, Male at no point contacted Hutchinson to thank him for his actions that day. My grandfather, like many of his generation, recognised the limitations that society had placed on his sons and daughters and tried to equip them as best he could, the tragedy being that, in so doing, he would irrevocably alter his relationship with his youngest son. British MPs from both sides of the house praise the country for being a meritocracy. Yet when confronted with the facts that hinder true equality, or levelling of the playing field, the onus is placed on Black citizens to keep repaying the debt of slave owners and racist notions that neither they nor their children were born into. As Bob Marley would sing, 'No chains around my feet but I'm not free.' The compensation for the emancipation of former slaves may have finally been paid off in 2015, but Black Britons are still paying the price for the legacy of British Empire. How free is a Black man in Britain in the twenty-first century?

5

Black Love is Radical

'I swipe right for everyone on Tinder ... except for Black girls.'

That was the conversation over dinner with a group of male friends who were all white. As others nodded in affirmation or chimed in with their comments of agreement, my shock steadily grew. I had known each of these men for over a decade. While we had sometimes had some disagreements around social stances or politics, this had never come up in conversation. Having learned how sensitive an issue race is, I tentatively tried to interrogate them about it. I was duly met with varying levels of offensiveness. 'They're just a bit much' and 'I don't mind mixed-race girls' to 'They're bare aggressive.'

Wait. *All* Black women?

'Obi, not everything is about race. Who wants another beer?'

I grappled in that moment with not wanting to cause a

scene, knowing that causing people to be on the defensive is one of the most sure-fire ways to ensure that neither one of you is truly listening or indeed likely to change the other's mind. With all that being said, I was trying to reconcile the men, who I deemed to be fair-minded, socially aware, critically thinking adults, with the seemingly close-minded obtuse views that they were espousing. Around the table, one by one, I began to hear the phrase 'it's just a personal preference' repeated, as each of my friends attempted to justify their dating history.

The past decade has seen a rise in dating apps, and with it the dating attitudes of the British people have been codified. This reduction to the language of tick boxes in every conceivable category has created a sense of personal tailoring and preference. However, as I was discovering, in society nothing exists in a vacuum – especially with regard to race. Gathering my thoughts, and another beer, I gently probed my friends as to who their teen crushes were and when did they remember first finding somebody attractive. Their answers were invariably the same: white girls and women from the TV shows and films they'd watched when they were younger. The trip down memory lane, lubricated by alcohol, brought to the fore forgotten names of breakfast hosts, girl band members and one particularly heated debate about who the hottest girl in the cast of *Friends* was. As I retreated from the back and forth over Rachel Green and Monica Geller, I scoured my own memory of the show for any Black women. The only notable character I could

think of was Ross's girlfriend, Dr Charlie Wheeler, portrayed by Aisha Tyler. How did a show that was set in New
York, which I had just returned from visiting, have such a
predominantly white cast? It didn't gel with my personal
experience of the city.

Before long, I was going down a rabbit hole in my mind.
As both an actor and avid consumer of all forms of recorded
media, I scoured my mind for a Black actress who played
the role of a romantic lead in a Hollywood film. Doubting
my memory, I asked my friends if they could think of any.
'There's loads ... there's Beyoncé ... what's her name from
12 Years a Slave [Lupita Nyong'o] ... oh, and Jessica Alba.'
As we scrambled to put together the names, I mulled over
the cause of our collective amnesia. In our assembling of
a handful of names, we had an actress who was predominantly seen as a singer, another whose best-known role at
the time was playing an enslaved woman who was violently
raped by a white man, and an actress with Latinx heritage
who they had confused as being of African descent. The
term 'personal preference' echoed resoundingly in my
thoughts as I tried to recall when my first crush appeared
and what exactly influenced it.

Growing up with two older brothers, I understandably
took my lead from them. Men's lifestyle magazines would
have features on gym workouts and cars that would lend
the pictures of the barely clothed women in the magazines
an air of respectability. My brothers' choice of magazine
guru was *FHM*, which from 1995 to 2017 published a list

of what it deemed '*FHM*'s 100 Sexiest Women'. Millions of votes were cast each year, as the magazine and the feature grew in popularity. In the more than twenty years that the feature ran, there were only four Black women who entered the top ten: Beyoncé, Ciara, Rihanna and Halle Berry, with the latter being the only Black woman ever to be awarded the title. For the most part, the women who were celebrated for being attractive by the media, advertisers and society at large looked a certain way.

Learning as I did from those around me, my 'personal preference' would be deeply impacted by what a majority white British media had decided was attractive. Certain body shapes and aesthetics were deemed 'fashionable' or 'hot', with typically 'African' features such as fuller lips or Afro hair seen as undesirable. Even as I looked at the list of Black actresses who featured in the top ten over the years, I was struck by the lack of dark-skinned Black women. Of the women who did appear on *FHM*'s list, many of them could be described as 'light-skinned Black women'. Though I was not aware of it at the time, those who were visibly lighter skinned seemed to benefit from a proximity to whiteness that both advertising and marketing executives found somehow more palatable. So when a spokesperson for *FHM* reflected that the list had 'helped propel the careers of many well-known actresses, musicians and models', I couldn't help but wonder whose career had been propelled and whose had been stunted. The word for the dynamic I was encountering is colourism.

Colourism is prejudice or discrimination against individuals with a dark skin tone, typically but not solely among people of the same ethnic or racial group. Mathew Knowles, father to pop icons Beyoncé and Solange, would make headlines when he called out the preferential treatment certain pop stars got in the music industry, saying, 'When it comes to Black females, who are the people who get their music played on pop radio? Mariah Carey, Rihanna, the female rapper Nicki Minaj, my kids. And what do they all have in common?' When the interviewer replied, 'They're all lighter skinned,' Knowles concluded, 'Do you think that's an accident?'

As lacking in diversity as some of the hit shows of the '90s and '00s were, especially considering where they were set, colourism and the idealised standards of beauty were not limited to white creative teams of casting directors, producers or directors. Kanye West, speaking to *Essence* magazine about his own personal preference in 2006, was quoted as saying, 'If it wasn't for race mixing, there'd be no video girls. Me and most of our friends like mutts a lot. Yeah, in the hood they call 'em mutts.' This internalised racism, misogyny and colourism is degrading to all Black women. Mathew Knowles, in stark contrast to Kanye West, was very much aware of his own internalised struggle with colourism, commenting that he believed when he first met her that Tina Knowles, future mother of Solange and Beyonce, was white. 'Later I found out that she wasn't, and she was actually very much in-tune with her Blackness.'

Coming to terms with his own childhood and the lessons he had internalised, he reflected, 'I had been conditioned from childhood with eroticised rage; there was actual rage in me as a Black man, and I saw the White female as a way, subconsciously, of getting even or getting back.'

Even as I internally chastised and attempted to hold the moral ground over my white friends for their own 'dating preferences', I began to unpick some of my own experiences and how they had brought me to where I was today. Ever since I had lost my virginity, I had been acutely aware that my sexuality and race were, despite my thoughts on the matter, implicitly linked. Only a few years later, that link would be made more explicit.

I first met Leah when I was eighteen years old in a central London pub. I had decided that I would be taking a gap year before applying to drama schools and attempting to begin a fledgling career as an actor. From the moment we locked eyes across the bar, the conversation sparked with an organic energy that felt electric, with neither one of us pausing for much thought. With pale white skin, fiery red hair and green eyes, she was nearly a foot shorter than me. The repartee flowed seamlessly, as we traded quips about her job working in PR and growing up near the border of Scotland. Before long, the intensity of the back and forth increased, and I found myself in a black cab accompanying her to her west London flat. The fact that she was eleven years older than me did not seem to daunt her in the slightest; in fact it was seen as an added bonus, apparently deeply flattering that she could still garner the attention of a younger man.

It was the beginning of one of the most significant relationships in my life. While I use the word relationship, I should clarify the parameters of our dynamic, as they were anything but usual. Relatively inexperienced as I was, I could hear my brother's years-old advice in my head: 'The main thing to do, is just listen. Whatever they want to do, be on board and go with it. But just listen. They'll tell you what they want.' Aware of the stark age gap between us, but also that we had undeniable chemistry, Leah was quite up front about her expectations.

'I don't mind what you get up to, as long as you're careful.'

'So, we're not exclusive?'

'I have no interest in fucking anyone else. I'm very happy with what I have here. But I understand you're a young man and you have desires.'

Having heard what she wanted, and knowing that it wouldn't limit me in any traditional sense, I saw no downside. Updating my schoolmates, who had been suddenly thrown into the whirlwind that is university fresher social life, many stated their envy at my having found an older woman to be my 'friend with benefits'. Casual drinks or company at the theatre were par for the course, after which we would spend the night together. It was the morning after one of these trips to the National Theatre that I pondered something borne of my own inexperience.

'So, is there anything you would like to try that you haven't? It could be anything,' I enquired as we lazed in bed.

'. . .'

'Go ahead. No judgement here. Honest.'

'I have this fantasy of a big Black guy taking me in the middle of the night.'

'How do you mean?'

'Just. You know. Stood at the base of my bed and in the middle of the night, waking me from my sleep and having his way with me. That moment of not knowing what is happening. Being disorientated and then . . . you know?'

Oh.

'I just think it would be hella hot.'

As I replay the dialogue in my head, I want to say that I interrupted the conversation. I want my eighteen-year-old self to be prepossessed enough to feel the same physical reaction I feel recollecting it. I want to say that I launched into a diatribe about how uncomfortable I was with stereotyping myself and tapping into the role of a sexually aggressive Black man having his way with a defenceless white woman in the dark and why it felt so offensive. That the offer of a spare key pressed into my hand so that I could enact the scenario whenever my oversexed Black male libido was roused was more dehumanising than she realised. That for the first time I felt that there were three of us now in whatever this unconventional relationship was. That I spoke out on the fact that now it felt like Leah, Obi and her idea of what a 'Black man' was and all that entailed were all present in that west London bedroom. I want to say that this offensive fetishising of my skin and my identity, conscious or not, was a buzzkill chastening me into abstaining from said situationship. I want to write that I didn't enjoy the role-play and the uniqueness of this dynamic. That it outraged me and didn't sit as a private little secret that I enjoyed, relishing in the taboo and forbidden nature of what I was participating in, feeling that it made me special. Unfortunately, the narrative that I had been taught about the little social currency that Black men have being tied to their sexuality meant that I was not inclined to divest myself of that perceived power, no matter the racist narratives that it was linked to. At the same time as I began to play out Leah's racist fantasy in my personal life, my professional life would eerily mirror it.

My first professional TV role as an adult was playing the part of Leslie 'Hutch' Hutchinson in the Channel 4 drama-documentary, *High Society's Favourite Gigolo*. Having recently turned eighteen and bracing myself for the 'real life' as an actor, I had very little idea what to expect. My first and only meeting for *Gigolo* was in the bar of a fancy hotel in Seven Dials, Covent Garden. Paul, the producer of the show, said at the end of our meeting, 'From the moment you walked in, you looked like you belonged here; that's going to be essential for this character. We don't normally get to be in places like this.'

It didn't have to be said; we both knew what was meant.

Paul was a handsome Black man in his early forties, suave in an understated way. Ordering himself a cocktail, and cutting through my polite declining, he pressed me into joining him with a mid-afternoon negroni. It had barely been five minutes before we began to speak with the old familiarity that can often confuse outsiders. I gratefully felt the layers of armour that I often feel necessary when talking to directors or producers, for them to view me as a professional, fall to the floor of the bar. The shorthand came thick and fast: gentle ribbing around the pronunciation of plantain, and to whether Jamaican or Nigerian cuisine is superior. He began to regale me with the tale of this West Indian musician who, in the 1920s and '30s, was Europe's highest-paid entertainer. A Grenadian jazz pianist and crooner who was a firm favourite of the then Prince of Wales, with heiress and socialite Edwina Mountbatten as a patron, he was a novelty and curiosity who soon became a recurrent feature at high society parties. 'He would finish a gig at Café de Paris or wherever and these ladies from high society would take him home ... and sometimes not just ladies.' Paul studied my face as he said this last sentence, in search of what, I'm not quite certain.

He continued to tell me all about this singer, Leslie Hutchinson, or 'Hutch', as he came to be called, his eyes brightening whenever the conversation returned to his protagonist; his navigating of spaces that 'they' may want you in *temporarily*, but in which you're always a guest. 'And yet, for all of that success, it was all temporary. He was caught having sex with a member of the royal family and the ensu-ing scandal ruined his career. White women, man! They'll fuck you up. It's all temporary.'

The thought stuck with me – that all too often unspoken awareness that being Black in Britain has always had a sense of impermanence. I recognised the familiar feeling of belonging through exclusion; the awareness of the outsider. It's the same awareness that linked Hutch, Paul and, to a certain extent, me. Where Leslie might have found himself forced to use servants' entrances to high-end establishments, Paul and I felt it in the subtler, quieter moments of looks that lingered too long and disapproving tuts at the exuberance of our laughter; our awareness of the conditional.

He began to talk me through the show, shot for shot and, bizarrely, for the first time I realised that I was the one being pitched to, sold the story of a character that seemed both glamorous and vulnerable. As an actor I had been under the impression that the norm is auditioning, selling oneself and ceding all power to directors, casting directors and producers; what was the catch? Paul steadied himself. 'It's been hard casting this role, man. Hutch didn't just have affairs with royalty like Edwina Mountbatten. He was indis-criminate about who he used his body to get ahead with.'

I am staring blankly waiting for the penny to drop. 'It was all kinds of white people.' I was missing something. 'He also had an affair with Cole Porter and we want to show that on screen.'

Cue another awkward pause. Paul seemed to be

anticipating a reaction from me that I wasn't being forth-coming with. Off of my vacant expression he pressed on: 'And that wouldn't be a problem for you? A gay kiss on screen? Because, and I'm assuming here, but you come across as a really straight dude ... and we've had four actors bail once they've realised that, you know ... ' The humbling fact that I wasn't even third or fourth choice for this role was replaced by dismay. Are Black actors really that bothered by portraying a bisexual man that they would turn down a job offer on prime-time terrestrial television?

'Obi! Come! You're on the TV. Hurry now.' Armed with a plate of jollof rice laden with fried plantain strewn across the top, I scurry from the kitchen into the jam-packed living room of my parents' Upper Holloway house with aunties, uncles and cousins perched on sofa edges and squeezed wherever they can find a seat. I am indeed on the television. The trailer for the source of this impromptu family gather-ing broadcasts on Channel 4 thirty minutes before the main event kicks off. I am cooed over by proud family members, as the tuxedo-attired freshly shaved 'Telly Obi' smooches with an older white woman while sat at a grand piano. The support for my desire to be an actor has been crowdsourced, if not financially funded, by the various branches of my extended family, with my parents organising family trips for aunts, uncles, cousins and family friends to watch some of my earliest theatrical performances.

As such, my professional debut on terrestrial television

is something that many of them feel personally invested in, though they have not been particularly interested in the specifics, per se. It is then perhaps a bit of a shock when, as the trailer for *High Society's Favourite Gigolo* comes to a close, 'Telly Obi' stands at the foot of a king-sized bed – being ogled by the same actress who is waiting expectantly in the bed – drops his robe and reveals a pair of naked buttocks to my family and whoever else is watching Channel 4 that November evening. There is gentle ribbing and teasing about how toned my butt looks.

'*Na wa o*! Look at this *naija nyash*!' declares my Aunt Lily to uproarious laughter that my parents' house has heard countless times before; the raucous familial back and forth. But the real shock comes a few minutes later, as Don Warrington narrates: 'Hutch had been brought up in a world where homosexuality was strictly taboo, but a pattern of opportunism began as he embarked on an affair with Porter that would prove highly beneficial to his career.' It is in that moment that Hutch, Paul and I united once again. The accompanying image of me topless next to a piano, leaning over and kissing an older white man with slicked back hair silences the room. The tension is palpable. I cast my mind back to that hotel meeting and Paul's difficulty in trying to cast the role. I ruminate on Hutch's willingness to be sexually open for his own career advancement, and in the midst of this I digest the thinly veiled horror on my extended family's face as they take in what has just happened.

I'm aware that this does not have seismic consequences

for my own sexuality or how I view it, but feel my hackles raise when the interrogation begins during the advert break. It comes from all sides: from Nigerian relations who have lived in London for decades and from those who have just moved to the UK.

'So, this is just you playing a part, right?'; '*Abi*, you couldn't have warned me before that I was going to be seeing . . . ?' my inquisitor tails off. My being leered over by an older white woman is something to laugh at, accompanied by comments of how I've 'always gone for cougars, you heartbreaker you'. But that suspension of disbelief, the ability to see a distinction between character and actor, evaporated when confronted with the apparently jarring image of a family member being so transgressive as to kiss another man.

During the tail end of my gap year, Leah would accept a job in Australia, and we would part ways just before I enrolled at the Drama Centre London to begin my three-year training to be a professional actor. The thematic connection that I felt between Hutchinson and myself subsided as I embarked on more conventional relationships that lacked the overt racial dynamics of my relationship with Leah. When the parallels did remerge they were stark in their similarities.

In the final year of my training at drama school, I was cast in a new translation of the Friedrich Dürrenmatt play, *The Physicists*, by Jack Thorne at London's Donmar Warehouse. It was my first professional role in London theatre and I would pinch myself most nights that I was lucky enough to be making a living doing what I had always dreamed of. I would leave the course at Drama Centre London early, leaping at the chance to have a head start in my professional career, a decision my tutors supported, using my performance in the show as my final assessment so that I would still be awarded my degree. My character was deliberately framed as a hulking brute of a figure, accentuated by a costume design of tight white trousers with matching T-shirt that might as well have been bought from Baby Gap for how much it suffocated the blood flow to my arms, which had been oiled to highlight any definition that I could bring to them throughout the run. Eager to please, and also keen to put my, pardon the expression, 'method acting' into place, I would spend the majority of the first act, during which I didn't have any lines, working out and lifting weights in my dressing room before coming on stage. The designer and director seemed content enough with the results, but it was my fellow actors who first pointed it out in the boys' dressing room: 'Mate, there are women in those aisles who are creaming themselves when you walk on stage. The stage manager will have a clean-up job on her hands.' As crude as the comment was, I noticed that there were occasionally audible gasps as I entered the stage lathered in baby oil. Soon enough, however, it would be more than just flattering sighs from audience members.

Theatres like the Donmar Warehouse have very little government funding. In a world of ever-increasing commercial

ticket prices and lavish budgets of the big West End theatres – which are used to attract the best actors, playwrights
and directors – it has always punched above its weight,
holding its own in the middle of Covent Garden. It is a tiny
250-seat theatre which should, by all rights, be dwarfed by
the neighbouring 1000-plus-seater behemoths of commer-
cially owned venues. Yet it continually produces some of
the most critically acclaimed work in the London theatre
tapestry. It has survived in large part due to the kindness
shown by philanthropists with a passion for the arts and by
companies looking to improve their outward-facing brand,
handing over large sums of money for the privilege of a few
face-to-faces with the actors over the course of the year. I had
long been an admirer of the Donmar, and as such was more
than happy to engage in any of these events, especially if it
made the security of the theatre's future more concrete. Yet
it was during one of these so-called 'donor dinners' that I
began to question at what price patronage comes.

After being whisked across the road from Seven Dials
into the heart of Soho by the fundraising team, my fellow
castmates and I were sat at a table with donors from the
bank and their spouses in an upstairs dining room of the
restaurant. The wine kept coming and the conversation
flowed just as easily. I found myself opposite one of the
bank donors while his wife sat to my right. A white couple
in their mid-forties, they moved quickly from pleasantries
about the show to their pursuit of a wide variety of passions.
I was regaled with tales of their arduous quest to perfect

wine made from grapes in their personal vineyard, and yoga retreats made to private islands by the wife; it was a life of luxury that my recent graduate actor ear listened to bemusedly. However, for all of the ease of our exchange, there was something unnervingly familiar about the way in which the conversation to and fro-ed. Whether it was a glance that would slowly morph into a gaze or a comment about how full my lips were, I found myself under the distinct impression that she was trying to hit on me.

For every beat of the conversation that could be deemed risqué – a comment enquiring about my workout regime and how happy she was with the results – there would be a correspondingly innocent comment about the most recent ballet she had attended. As flattered as I was by the attention of this glamorous quadragenarian, I found myself self-consciously checking in with her husband to ensure that this potential flirtation wasn't some horrendous faux pas; that I wasn't engaging in something dangerous with the very people who were helping to fund our show. As it was, the dinner came to an end, and not a moment too soon, with the parting comment from the lady in question complimenting me on how smooth my 'mocha skin' looked and enquiring what moisturiser I used. We said our goodbyes and I made my excuses with a trip to the gents before I headed out. At which point my evening took a turn.

I was just washing my hands when the husband entered the bathroom. After a cursory glance around, he thanked me for a lovely evening and for such a splendid show.

Bashful as I always am in instances such as these, when I feel undeserving of praise, I smiled courteously and made to leave. It was then that I realised he wasn't using any of the facilities; his body position in front of the door and a glint in his eye implied a desire to get something off of his chest and that I wouldn't be leaving until we'd had our conversation. My thoughts flashed back to the dinner table and a primal fear began to grip me. The frisson of our conversation had not gone unnoticed or, it appeared to me now, disregarded. My naïve mind jumped to a variety of conclusions with several permutations, but with one underlying outcome: what had begun as an innocent, sociable dinner had taken a dangerous turn, and by tomorrow morning my agent would receive a call that I had been recast and was off of the show. The husband locked eyes with me and, considering me for a second, with a soft voice told me:

'My wife and I are making an evening of it and are staying at a hotel very nearby.' I smiled, slightly thrown, unsure of what to make of his and his wife's sleeping arrangements. 'She seems *very* taken with you. I wonder if you would join us back at our hotel for the evening. Of course we would be very discreet, but it would be our pleasure.'

I stood, silent. Unsure how to take this new development, I merely stared.

In an attempt to put me at ease, he continued: 'I would not *have* to be involved, if that is what you're worried about. We've never had a Black companion; I would be content just to watch if that's something you would be more comfortable with.'

He was so sure, so confident. I had no response. Just more silence.

Perhaps testing the patience and impulses of a man who worked in finance, he said, now more assertively, 'Of course we would make it worth your while. Would one thousand work?'

I realised I had to say something, had to engage in the situation. 'That is … deeply flattering,' I fumbled, 'but I have an incredibly early start tomorrow morning. I should be responsible and try and get an early night.'

His eyes narrowed on me, sizing me up as one might a vendor at a street market, unsure how far their resolve will hold. 'Money is not an issue, but we would both enjoy sharing your company tonight. Would two thousand be sufficient?' I tittered, trying to give off the impression of being bashful and humble so as not to feel too angry about being accosted in this way. It was slowly beginning to dawn on me just quite what was being suggested, and the fear I'd felt merely moments ago was being replaced with a bubbling ire. I reasoned that my first port of call had to be exiting this situation as swiftly as possible with as few words as possible.

'Honestly, I would normally love to, and it has been a pleasure meeting you both, but I should probably go.'

Whatever finality I had managed to infuse into my tempered turndown seemed to do the trick, greeted as I was by a face that looked more quizzically disappointed that he hadn't gotten what he wanted, than affronted by my refusal to spend the evening having sex with his wife. 'The pleasure has most definitely been ours; but that it had been more . . . '

I found myself on the streets of Soho, my conscious mind slowly becoming cognisant of what had just happened. I realised I had been flying by the seat of my pants, falling back on learned notions of code-switching and politeness to extricate myself from a potentially dangerous situation. Shards of conversation began flooding back, compounding my rising fury like a Tetris board unable to compute each moment in context.

'Mocha skin'. 'Wonderful arms'. 'Black companion'.

As palatable as each of these comments felt in the moment, only raising the vaguest of flags, amorphous in isolation, united they solidified and compacted to turn the overpriced dinner and copious wine in my stomach to bile. My first thought, to my shame, was that I had considered it. Being a small subsidised theatre in town, the Donmar at the time was not paying its actors fabulously well, relying more on the promise of great work than of a healthy bank balance. The result was that my take home pay after my agent's commission and various taxes did not amount to much more than £350 a week. That my entire take-home pay for the run of performances could be nearly matched by somebody for whom money was no object? Fine. You are a struggling artiste, Obi. This is what you signed up for. But my body? My consent? Could it be mitigated? Should it be mitigated? After all, I was a single man in my early twenties. What difference did it make to me? Why not make some money? All of us actors had to some degree been selling ourselves that evening; giving up our time to make a bunch of rich people feel a bit more incentivised to part with their money and commit to our project. And she was beautiful. I had thought it myself, had flirted and enjoyed it. So was I really that bothered about selling my body to somebody who was willing to pay me such gross amounts of money? No, it was the elephant in the room. The true glue that bonded this indignity together was the specificity of the request.

'We have never had a Black companion.'

Suddenly, the rest of the evening had come into sharp relief; every glance, every comment about my physical shape, my hair, my skin. Each interaction became retrospectively scrutinised. I wasn't just 'Obi' in that moment. Something about *my* sexuality in that room felt like a commodity to be enjoyed, experienced and discussed at dinner tables like a yoga retreat or a wine from a private vineyard. The tension between how unique I was as a young mixed-race man in a room full of white men and women, and the totemic nature of what I represented to this couple, hopeful I would fulfil their expectations of what a 'Black man' was, left me with a sense of unease in my own skin. The complexity of my identity didn't matter. Just like Leah, and just like my first girlfriend before her, I represented 'Blackness' to them. I was Black enough. *Exotic* enough.

Perhaps it was the locale, my proximity to that very same Covent Garden hotel in which I'd had drinks with Paul that stirred the memory, but the homogeneity of the experience as Black men working in the entertainment industry did not escape me. The transactional nature of what I could offer this rich, white couple echoed my dramatised portrayal of Hutch. For some casual spending money for them, I could give them the fulfilment of their idea of experiencing a Black body, specifically a 'Black man'. The dreaded impact of what denying this might do to my career, real or imagined, was a very present threat in my mind. Hutch was a man who had felt the weight of personal scandal on his professional career, knocking him from heights very few could have imagined, considering the daily occurrences of racism he experienced; all because he had slept with a married royal white woman. He was acutely aware of the double-edged sword that being a hypersexualised Black man entailed. In a crystalising moment, so was I. So there I was, a bottle of wine to the good, having an existential crisis in the middle of Soho. In a world where personal preference had become so normalised, was there any harm in choosing to monetise or commodify my sexuality? And was I wrong to be offended by those who sought to commodify me?

Where I began to feel an increasing sense of discomfort about being fetishised by the opposite sex, several of my Black peers felt entirely comfortable with having their race and masculinity venerated. In the horror film *Get Out*, a film that feels very much in conversation with *Guess Who's Coming to Dinner*, a young Black man, Chris, finds himself trapped in 'the sunken place' after visiting the family of his white girlfriend, Rose Armitage. Chris is one of several Black men in the film to find themselves trapped in a fugue-like state by Rose's mother, who uses a cup of tea to hypnotise them. It becomes apparent that the Armitages have been using Rose to lure exclusively Black people to the house so that they might use them for their own nefarious ends.

The self-awareness of the potentially problematic racial dynamic many Black men feel in interracial relationships was epitomised by a tweet a British Yoruba friend of mine, Seun, posted shortly after watching the film: 'I know I should get out of the #SunkenPlace but I just can't quit my Custard Cream! #GetOut.'

Whereas Seun knew for certain that there was a racial dynamic to his relationship that he probably *should* address and interrogate, he wanted to enjoy his 'personal preference' of his white partner, whom he would compare to a 'Custard Cream', blindfolding himself to any of the more problematic racial dynamics at play.

The internalised racism that Mathew Knowles spoke of seemed very much at play in Britain, and arguably the over-sexualisation of Black men could not be found more publicly than by the all-Black male touring strip show, 'The Chocolate Men'. The subject of the Channel 4 documentary, *The Black Full Monty*, the group's co-directors Dante Aaron-Williams and Louis 'Legacy' Francois openly admit, 'We're selling a fantasy.' The trope that the group is exploiting is that of insatiable, over-sexed, hyper-masculine, cis-gendered

Black men who not only must be in top physical shape but also have a penis that measures a minimum of eight inches. Francois states candidly in the documentary, 'That's why you're coming to the show. You are coming to see big Black willies.' Echoing Knowles's sentiments regarding internalised racism, one performer – given the name Django by Dante and Louis because of his African heritage – asserted, 'Here in Britain we are at the bottom of the food chain ... this is me taking my power back.'

Despite the fact that there seemed to be women of all ethnicities in the audiences, the documentary focused largely on the white women, with one Dubliner justifying her attendance: 'Think of the years that we've suffered or tolerated women being objectified. It's nice to kind of turn it around and enjoy the male form in vulgarity and in an obnoxious nature.'

The fears that had been stoked about Black men in Britain for centuries as a threat towards white women has been reclaimed by some women who found agency in subverting narratives about their sexual passivity, discovering that there were certain Black men who would be all too willing participants in an interesting dance that I consistently found myself at the centre of. The American author and activist bell hooks, commenting on this phenomenon, wrote:

White women and Black men have it both ways. They can act as oppressor or be oppressed. Black men may be victimized by racism, but sexism allows them to act as exploiters and oppressors of women. White women may be victimized by sexism, but racism enables them to act as exploiters and oppressors of Black people ... As long as these two groups or any group defines liberation as gaining social equality with ruling class white men, they have a vested interest in the continued exploitation and oppression of others.

My uncovering of the insidiousness of the underlying foundations to many of my own relationships forced me to interrogate the narratives I had consumed about Black women. Despite Django's assertions in the documentary that Black men were 'bottom of the food chain', the glaring omission of Black women was telling. I remembered my friends' assertions that Black women were 'bare aggressive', and thought about my earliest memories of depictions of Black women. Besides the 'mammy' trope, of a larger, older, dark-skinned woman who is amiable and maternal, the other dominant stereotype is that of the 'angry and/or sassy Black woman' or 'sapphire'. These women are often seen to be aggressive, physically dominant and constantly criticising Black men for either being unemployed or sleeping with white women. Pondering my own media consumption, my mind was drawn to the film I took my teenage date to see, on my first-ever date: *Save The Last Dance.* The film tells the story of a young white ballet dancer who moves to an inner-city school on the south side of Chicago and still harbours hopes of going to Juilliard School, a world-renowned performing arts conservatory in New York City. Befriending a Black girl called Chenille, she soon strikes up a relationship with Chenille's brother Derek. Not everybody approves of the interracial relationship, however – namely Derek's ex-girlfriend and, latterly, Chenille herself.

'You and Derek act like it don't bother people to see you together. Like it don't hurt people to see.'

'Well, we like each other. What is the big damn deal? It's me and him, not us and other people.'

'Black people, Sara. Black women. Derek's about something. He's smart. He's motivated. He's for real. He's not gonna make babies and not take care of them, or run the streets messing up his life. He's gonna make something of himself. And here you come – white, so you gotta be right – and take one of the few ... decent men we have left after jail, drugs and drive-by. That is what Nikki meant about you up in our world.'

Although I was too young to notice it at the time, much like *Guess Who's Coming to Dinner*, the acceptable interracial coupling as lead characters seemed to be a Black man and a white woman. Framing the Chenille character as having prejudiced attitudes precludes the couple from having to explore their own desirability and respectability politics.

The same clichéd framing of Black women as hypercritical of and an obstacle to Black men's sex lives was apparent in my rewatching of *Sex and the City* almost a decade later.

Despite being set in New York City in the '00s, where 35 per cent of the population were non-white, of the 95 dating partners that the four girls have, only three of them are non-white: two Black men and one Hispanic woman. In the uncomfortable viewing that is Season Three's 'No Ifs, Ands or Butts', Samantha brags to the rest of her friends that she is sleeping with Chivon, the Black brother of her colleague Adeena, and that he does indeed have a 'big Black cock', while simultaneously bragging that she 'doesn't see colour; only conquests'. When Adeena informs her she 'has a problem with [her] only brother getting serious with a white woman', and advises her to break it off, Samantha refuses to back down and a fight breaks out. After Chivon tells Samantha that he is siding with his sister, a concluding voiceover narrates, 'Samantha knew the real problem wasn't her little white pussy; it was the fact that Chivon was a big Black pussy who wouldn't stand up to his sister.'

As I ruminated on my own dating history, I wondered how the consistent narrative around Black women and their desirability had warped my perceptions.

My own attempts at dating had been floundering. Having parents who had been married for over thirty years, despite initial opposition from my grandparents, had set unrealistic expectations for me about what True Love™ could and should be. While a recent survey concluded that almost a third of relationships start at work, my workplaces were almost exclusively white. London, just like New York, is a very diverse city and, as of 2011, more than 40 per cent of the population was non-white. After two decades of being taught that my social and sexual value was linked to my race, was it a mere coincidence that I had ended up with a dating past that was predominantly white? A personal preference? And did my evolving grappling with my identity necessitate a reordering of my dating priorities?

At the age of twenty-four, I attended my first West African wedding. It was between my friend Kojo and his wife-to-be Alice. Although the bride and groom were Ghanaian and not Nigerian, the pastor's sermon felt familiar. Having grown up with family members and friends who were Evangelical Christians, I was no stranger to non-Catholic sermons. But as I watched my two friends getting married, I felt uncomfortable listening to the pastor.

'Just as at home in the village, the woman knows that the man knows best, so in the church, the wife recognises that the husband knows best. He is the surgeon, she is the nurse.'

The nods of affirmation and titters from my elders around me didn't surprise me. What did was that my Black contemporaries, men and women, were echoing 'Amen'. But this was not my culture per se, nor was it the time or the place to have a debate, so I bit my tongue until we were sitting down for the evening meal. When the topic of the sermon resurfaced, it was a cousin of Kojo's, Adjoa, a Ghanaian doctor I was seated next to, who voiced her consternation.

'Listen, if my fiance ever let me be called a 'nurse' in front of our friends and family? Game over. Period.'

A male relative on the table chimed in, 'But it's just part of the culture. It's not even that deep.'

'Bun the culture. I didn't spend a decade in training to marry someone who would allow such a disrespect to who I am as a person. That ain't the culture for me.'

Growing up, I was friends with a British-born Nigerian girl and her brother, who was fourteen months younger than her. He could and did date whoever he chose and was allowed to bring his numerous girlfriends to their parents' house, where they would invariably spend the night. She, however, was told explicitly that she couldn't bring *anybody* home unless that man was her fiancé. As he sat watching the football on Sky Sports, it was his sister's job to prepare the dinner for the family. When food was served, culture dictated that the men in the house were served first.

Dating for her was a minefield. When approached by a white guy, she would receive the unsolicited 'compliments' that she was 'pretty for a Black girl', or that the man 'had never been with a Black girl before'. Having been on the receiving end of these comments several times, she had grown quite skilled in filtering out the non-Black prospective partners who held problematic attitudes. Despite that, she recalled feeling that she needed to stop seeing one of her white exes when, mid-coitus, he called her his 'African queen'. Although they connected on several levels, race felt like such a key part of her identity that having it romanticised and fetishised was an insurmountable obstacle.

Regrettably, she found that Black men also struggled

with problematically racialised views of Black women. Were she to express an interest in a prospective Black partner, she would often hear rebuttals along the lines that they 'weren't ready for something serious'. When she asked me why, as a Black man, I didn't typically date Black women, I was stumped. She didn't mean it to, but it caused a swell of guilt. The moral high ground I'd felt I occupied during the wedding service evaporated. I tried to self-rationalise: my dual heritage, I told myself, had made dating more nuanced for me and race didn't really affect me in the same way. Even as I thought it, I could hear the fragility of the argument. Dating for her brother, however, seemed less complex. When I asked him why he exclusively dated white girls, his answer was, 'They're just easier, plus I'm just not ready for my queen yet. I probably will when I'm older.'

Unfortunately, being Black does not make you immune to being racist, just as being a woman doesn't mean you don't internalise misogynist values. The feminist scholar and activist Moya Bailey coined the term *misogynoir* to describe the misogyny directed at Black women, where both race and gender play a role in the bias Black women experience. The very specific expectations and pressures put on Black women by their own community is just one instance of misogynoir. Often the expectation is that they will wait to eventually be a wife and mother to a Black man, palmed off with platitudes about their exulted worth; their sexuality and femininity glorified with descriptions like 'Nubian goddess' and 'queen'.

Speaking of a trip back to Nigeria to see relatives, my friend recounted being told by her aunt that she had gotten 'too dark' after tanning while travelling, recommending to her the body lotion 'Fair and Lovely'. Sadly, the attitudes of her aunt are not unusual: in 2011, the World Health Organisation reported that 77 per cent of Nigerian women use skin-lightening products on a regular basis. Not only have we absorbed and internalised a European ideal of beauty and romance through the media, we have also witnessed a double standard that our parents reinforced. Regardless of the individual sexual agency of Black women, the cultural education we received in the 1990s from within our community was that there was one rule for Black boys and another for Black girls. Black girls are taught to see the opposite sex as superiors who, under the guise of tradition, are to be deferred to, whether in a romantic or familial setting. Similarly to other patriarchal cultures around the world, in Igbo culture, regardless of how many daughters have come before, special preference is given to the first-born son, or the *okpara*. The burden of responsibility to the rest of the family falls on his shoulders, no matter his ability or suitability to bear such a burden. Men are expected to be the breadwinners, while women will take care of home affairs. That, of course, does a disservice to both parties.

The more I think back to the wedding discourse, the more my sympathies grow for Adjoa. She had been raised to excel academically to achieve the grades necessary to become a doctor. She was also caught negotiating a double bind of not wanting to be at the behest of racist ideas about her beauty from white partners, but also aware that many Black men felt intimidated or emasculated by an intelligent woman whose talents had grown beyond that of the domestic role culturally expected of her.

In a conversation discussing Black love recorded in London in 1971, the writers Nikki Giovanni and James Baldwin enacted a role-play, examining the fear of emasculation that Black men in a predominantly white and racist society feel and their inability to make Black women feel supported in the same conditions.

NIKKI GIOVANNI: And what does the truth matter?
Why you gonna be truthful with me when
you lie to everybody else? You lied when you
smiled at the cracker down at the job. Right?
Lie to me! Smile! Treat me the same way you
would treat him.

JAMES BALDWIN: I can't treat you the same way I
would treat him.

NIKKI GIOVANNI: You must! You must! Because
I've caught the frowns and the anger. He's
happy with you. Of course he doesn't know
you're unhappy. You grin at him all day long.
You come home and I catch hell. Because I
love you, I get the least of you; I get the very
minimum. And I'm saying, you know, fake

it with me. Is that too much for the Black
woman to ask of the Black man?

The misogynoir that Black women are subjected to from
both within and outside of the Black community is regrettably not limited to their romantic lives. Throughout history,
on both sides of the Atlantic, Black women have played
oversized roles in community organising and fighting
for causes in which Black people are disproportionately
affected. Even as Black women shoulder a disproportionate
amount of responsibility to effect change and combat racism
and sexism, their apparent natural allies in Black men have
often fallen short in reciprocating such support.

Black women, and in particular Stacey Abrams, had
praise heaped upon them in the US presidential elections
of 2020 for spearheading the drive to register more than
800,000 new voters to repudiate the regressive policies,
misinformation, toxic language and attacks on the media
that had come from The White House in the preceding
four years. Abrams and the other Black women who organised to combat voter suppression rightfully deserve much
credit. However, accepting that the onus to 'save American
democracy' – as one *Vogue* article posited when profiling
Abrams – falls on the shoulders of Black women comes
dangerously close to absolving those who have historically had the power to effect change of their responsibility
to do so. Demanding that Black women summon saintly
levels of determination, strength and fortitude because

it is somehow an inherent part of their nature is a racist narrative that not only sees them painted as 'aggressive' or 'a bit much', but can also have very real life dangers and health implications.

A report into maternal morbidity from researchers at Oxford University in November 2019 found that Black women are five times more likely than white women to die in pregnancy, childbirth or the postpartum period. This statistic had consistently been written off as Black women being at a higher risk of conditions causing high blood pressure, such as pre-eclampsia. However, one senior midwife and policy advisor, Janet Fyle, believes that underlying prejudices about Black women lie at the heart of the matter. 'Black women are categorised according to a white perspective; they are not believed. This notion of them having a higher threshold for pain and these biases mean that we miss serious conditions or the opportunity to escalate serious changes in the woman's condition in a timely way.'

As grateful as I am for the tremendous efforts consistently made by Black women, a narrative that paints them as invincible Kryptonians who do not need due love, support and care themselves is a burden they should never have to bear.

When a British-Nigerian friend of mine, Chinemeze, married his fellow British-Nigerian sweetheart, it was no surprise to any of his friends and family. They had a traditional Igbo wedding and, before long, their first child was born. It was here that the problems began. Chinemeze's wife had a very well-paid job in the City, far out-earning his comparatively modest estate agent salary. However, when they announced that he would be a stay-at-home dad, the reaction of their families varied from making disapproving comments to openly castigating him at family gatherings for being the chef. Despite the financial and emotional sense it made for him, he was seen to be neutering himself by not being the main earner. He was constantly battling both his own family and in-laws for his Black masculinity to be seen on his own terms.

As a doting father, Chinemeze believed he had found a renewed purpose in life while his wife was promoted through the ranks. The constant critiques of the couple's choice, however, would lead to Chinemeze battling situational depression. 'It took a long time for me to realise,' he confided in me, 'and then even after I had realised, it took me even longer to admit. I felt such a deep shame that I needed therapy. But I was so low. I had had no idea of the cumulative cut each of the snide remarks had on me. Like, just let me live.'

Ultimately, after he was encouraged by his wife and therapist to speak candidly with his parents and siblings about how their opinions were affecting him, they began to accept the familial set up that they had initially deemed unconventional. Suicide is the largest killer of men under the age of forty-five, with an average of thirteen men taking their life every day in England and Wales, according to figures from the Office of National Statistics in 2018. These findings seem to make tragic sense in a world that heaps pressure on men to assume certain financial responsibilities, irrespective of their partner's job prospects.

In Chinemeze and his wife, I saw something radical in their rejection of the roles that were culturally expected of them. In a world that painted Black men as sexually voracious and in pursuit of the ideal of beauty that was white Western women, his constancy in marrying a Black woman he had known since his childhood struck me as an exception. 'She just sees me, man. Like, she knows what I'm about. I'm not trying to be anything. We're just easy in each other's company. She sees me.'

My thoughts turned once more to the onscreen representation and images of Black love. Barry Jenkins's 2018 film adaptation of the James Baldwin novel *If Beale Street Could Talk* would feel revolutionary. The film is a tender, passionate, hard-hitting story of Fonny, a young Black man falsely accused and imprisoned on a charge of rape, and his partner, Tish. While some moments in the film are by turn shocking and heartbreaking, at its core Baldwin's writing is centred on the journey of self-discovery that a young couple, newly in love, go on together. Living in a racist society can by no means be excised from the context of the film, but Jenkins's focus was on sharing a narrative that was missing from the cultural landscape. 'For me, all I can do is not be concerned about filling the vacuum and just try to do the best I can to tell these stories in the way they demand to be told.'

His lead actor, Stephan James, would agree. 'It's crazy that in 2019 we say, "Wow, this [a Black love story] looks different", but we never get to see it. Part of the appeal of being in a film like this was understanding that this idea of Black love doesn't exist because we never see it ever. To show Black people as more than lovers, more than best friends, to show them as true soul mates – there's real power in that.'

Interrogating the attitudes of my friends, and my own, I was becoming starkly aware not only of how limiting and restrictive narratives around Black men had been, but also how this had led men of all ethnicities to treat Black women. A reluctance to show Black women in their complexity and depth in the broader media, coupled with a cultural bias to elevate the status of men from within my own community, had led me to internalise racist narratives about who I found desirable. As much as I wanted to believe in the choice of 'personal preference', I could not ignore the narratives I had absorbed growing up. This led me to two uncomfortable questions. Firstly, was I, as a Black man, guilty of leaning into the fetishisation I had experienced from white women? And secondly, was I prepared to divest myself of the perceived power it had given me? The answer to the first question, as my experiences had demonstrated, and as awkward as it was to admit to

173

myself, was a resounding yes. The answer to the second would lead me to unpick a lifetime of internalised narratives and question how prepared I was to unlearn, change and ultimately grow.

6

The Un-Blackness of Queerness

'Okay, well, let me turn that back around on you. When did you first know that you were one hundred per cent unequivocally straight?'

I'm sat across from my old school friend Anthony, or, as I've known him for the best part of two decades, Trish (his nickname). Suddenly I'm thrown.

'I dunno. I guess ... I'd never ... yeah, I guess I just never ... I've always known.'

'Same here.'

The idea of my being anything other than heterosexual was never entertained in my household. Not that my parents said anything explicitly; just that it wasn't expected. Cooed over by older relatives and family friends, my propensity to smile and my cheerful disposition led them to comment, 'Ooh, he's gonna be breaking all the girls' hearts soon enough.' It was taken as a given that I was straight, and any deviation from that felt like both a slight and a personal attack. Even before the unseemly incident of me violently retaliating to being called a homophobic slur in primary school, older foster siblings would jovially tease me about whether I had a girlfriend yet and where would I take her out on a date. Comments closer to home from my brother about my Irish dancing classes, or from James about my music choices, connected the dots in my mind.

Just as I had scrambled to find myself represented on screen, what I saw in the media I consumed was not only that heterosexuality was perceived to be the norm, but also that it was a failing of a man to even be suspected of being gay. The homophobic jokes that populated the *Scary Movie* franchise and Seth Rogen's earlier works, such as *Superbad* and *40-Year-Old Virgin*, and the consistent use of 'gay panic' in TV shows like *Friends*, made clear to me that to be gay was something of a joke, to be avoided at all costs. In exploring my identity and grappling with my place in a world that had racialised me as non-white, I found myself gravitating towards the more visible lynchpins of Black culture from within the diaspora – namely music.

Hip-hop, R&B, bashment and dancehall, grime and reggae: these were the genres played on pirate stations and blasted from loudspeakers at Notting Hill Carnival. The more I was versed in this music, the greater my social clout. James, or 'Big J', and I would stay up late in each other's rooms, writing and testing out adolescent raps, which I would then unveil in the school playground. I witnessed my standing increase as I challenged other pubescent poets to battles. I began to lose track of whether spitting bars, clashing other playground MCs and learning street dance routines was what I genuinely wanted to do or whether I did these things because they were what I thought was expected of me. With the top grime MCs of the day such as Kano and Wiley battling each other in a series of clashes entitled 'Lord of the Mic' as my inspiration, I penned verses that boasted of my sexual prowess and demeaned my unnamed opponents' lack of success with women. I sought to emulate some of the best rappers at the time and was not alone in purchasing and committing to memory several verses of the discography of Marshall Mathers (more commonly known by his stage name Eminem), in particular the soundtrack to the semi-autobiographical *8 Mile*, about a white Detroit battle-rapper. I knew better than to target any of my friends and peers with the affronting language, but nevertheless the homophobic epithets would roll off of my tongue with disturbing ease as I tried to impress my fellow classmates with my unrivalled mimicry.

Though in later years I would outgrow listening to the offending records, Mathers would show an unwillingness to change paths in the face of decades-long criticism. In 2013, a stubborn Mathers would defend his insistence on the use of the word 'faggot' when asked about it for *Rolling Stone*.

'It was more like calling someone a bitch or a punk or asshole. So that word was just thrown around so freely back then. It goes back to that battle, back and forth in my head, of wanting to feel free to say what I want to say, and then [worrying about] what may or may not affect people.' Mathers' defence would perhaps have rung less hollow if his mastery of the English language had not allowed him the restraint to censure himself from uttering other words.

Despite being in an industry that is heavily populated with African-Americans who consistently use the 'N-word', Mathers has yet to record a track using the slur. One can hardly claim that Dr Dre or 50 Cent, frequent collaborators of Mathers, do not 'throw the word around freely'. Mathers knows that it would be career suicide for him to use the N-word in any context; homophobia apparently less so. Although Mathers' lyrics are plainly derogatory, they were hardly outliers. In a candid interview in 2005, Kanye West summed up the homophobia that pervaded the industry: 'Everybody in hip-hop discriminates against gay people ... matter of fact the exact opposite word of hip-hop I think is gay.'

I would not truly realise the full extent of my reckless parroting of this language until called out by a close friend. It was after a play rehearsal for a show I was performing in during my gap year that one of my fellow castmates, Duane, hearing that I was taking public transport, offered me a lift home in his car. Duane had grown up in Tottenham, and in the first week of rehearsals we had bonded over our shared passion for music, choosing Sean Paul and Beyoncé to warm up to. It was perhaps this shared affinity for music that encouraged him to make me resident DJ for the car journey back to north London. Although we were the only two

Black members of the cast, his family hailed from Jamaica. As I was scrolling through my iPod searching for the best songs to continue the sing-a-long and car-seat choreography, I queued up my next choice, *Chi-Chi Man* by T.O.K. Certain that Duane knew the song, I waited for him to join in. When he did not, I sung all the more confidently, hoping I might jog his memory and participation. I was halfway through the chorus and skanking in the passenger seat when Duane icily interrupted me.

'Yeah, Obi, I beg you turn this off.'

I laughed, nervously. 'Are you joking?'

He turned to me with a face of stone. 'Does it look like I am laughing to you?'

I pulled the aux cable out and heard static as the wire rested against the joystick, the low hum of the jack the only thing breaking the silence between us. After what felt like an eternity, as we hit a red light, Duane turned and looked at me.

'I thought you were cool, G. How are you gonna play that?'

'It's a tune. I just thought—'

'Hold up.' I could sense I had agitated him again.

'What do you think this song is about?' he asked, as he pulled the car over to the side of the road.

I shrugged sheepishly. For as long as I had heard the song, and as often as I had danced to it at house parties, the West Indian patois had been indecipherable to me. Lacking lyric sheets to learn the words, I had just enjoyed the music and not paid it a second thought.

'It's about burning gay people or "chi-chi men" to death in their cars and in their clubs. Still think it's a "tune"? Dancing out to watching a brudda like me burn?'

I was mute. I tried searching for the words, but none were forthcoming. Every sentence I started seemed inadequate, falling short of the chasm I had opened up between us in the early days of our friendship.

'I'm sorry.'

The keys now pulled out of the ignition, Duane studied my face.

'You really didn't know?'

'The accent is thick. I was just enjoying the vibe. I'm so sorry.' I paused before admitting, 'I didn't even know you were gay.'

'Why should that matter?'

The bluntness of the question would stump me for days. The mental gymnastics I had engaged in as I thought over regurgitated defences about homophobic lyrics suddenly felt flimsy. As painful and as awkward as my search for my identity had been, my sexuality had never been a point of contention or even discussion. There was never really a moment when I had to choose or make a statement about who I was attracted to. I guess I've always known.

I'm back sitting across from Anthony.

'Same here. You're watching *Saved by the Bell* and you know that you fancy Zach. I'm not even in secondary school yet, but I know that I'm watching Zach more than I'm watching Kelly.

You just know that you're different and you try to suppress that. It would take me years to find myself. But as I found the other boys in our year who were queer, hanging around the music department, I began to feel more comfortable.'

Anthony and I went to school together from the age of eleven and have stayed friends since. Although we didn't take many classes together, as one of the choral scholars, I would be found at most hours in the music department. For Anthony and other queer boys in our year, the faculty would provide a de facto safe space. The unashamed flamboyant nature of their teaching style would lead to muttering from the class that 'I swear sir is so gay, man!' as teenage preoccupation with the social life of teachers grew to fever pitch. The consequence of having an adult presence that might be gay meant that the frequency and boldness with which pupils would launch homophobic insults at fellow students greatly diminished. This was something that would not go unnoticed or unappreciated by Anthony.

'I felt like I had a personality disorder. You know what it's like, being Black in a work environment; you feel you have to talk more professionally, dress a certain way, act a certain way to pre-empt being called "aggressive". It was like that for me at school, but worse. My voice can't be camp; I have to change it from a tenor to a bass. I can't swing my hips. I need to make sure my wrist isn't cocked. In any one day, I could be three or four different people. It gave people the chance to mock me, so eighty per cent of the time I would try to act straight.'

Unfortunately for Anthony, and for all of our

contemporaries, many teachers felt hamstrung in offering support to gay students and countering homophobic narratives due to Britain's first new homophobic law to be introduced in a century – the controversial Section 28. The law was a Local Government Act that stated that schools 'shall not intentionally promote homosexuality or publish material with the intention of promoting homosexuality' or 'promote the teaching in any maintained school [state school] of the acceptability of homosexuality as a pretended family relationship'. Capitalising on the lack of knowledge available at the emergence of the AIDS crisis, and the stigma attached to gay men in particular, right-wing news outlets ran aggressively homophobic headlines such as 'Britain Threatened by Gay Virus Plague' from the *Mail on Sunday*, while *The Sun* opted for 'Gay and Wicked'.

Research in 1987 went on to show that 75 per cent of the British public believed that 'homosexuality was always or mostly wrong'. Gay rights would be high on the political agenda before the General Election of 1987, and Labour's fractious position on the issue would prove helpful for the Conservative Party, who took the election in a landslide victory. The law was passed by the Prime Minister, Margaret Thatcher, who voiced her opposition to gay rights at the Conservative Party conference later that year.

'Children who need to be taught to respect traditional moral values are being taught that they have an inalienable right to be gay. All of those children are being cheated of a sound start in life. Yes, cheated.'

Although there were never any prosecutions under Section 28, it would be fifteen years before the Labour government finally repealed it, though the repeal would not receive unanimous political support. In 2000, one year before being elected as an MP, David Cameron would accuse Prime Minister Tony Blair of being 'anti-family' and legislating for the 'promotion of homosexuality in schools'. In 2003, he voted against its repeal. The vague language of the law put teachers in the uncomfortable position of deciding what could and should be taught in the classroom and how far a teacher could go in reprimanding students for using homophobic language. One of my former teachers would tell me, 'It just ran through the school. It could be an open secret, but it was a case of "don't ask, don't tell".' For Anthony, this confusion meant that he didn't feel he could rely on teachers to protect him from abuse on a day-to-day basis.

'I would get it from people in our year. But once we had all hit puberty and found each other, it kind of died down, because we had our clique. You had the rugby lot, the music lot, the gays etc. But what really hurt was from the years below. Kids two, three years younger than us thinking it was acceptable or 'cool' to throw the F-bomb at you. And we're Nigerian. You know how it is.'

Unfortunately, I did. The legacy of the British Empire in Africa extended far beyond the pillaging of natural resources and the forced labour of African people to work on slave plantations on the other side of the Atlantic Ocean. In justifying its subjugation of citizens throughout the

Empire, and later the British Commonwealth, the dehuman-isation of the indigenous populations was key. From the Americas to Africa and Asia and Australasia, the rhetoric of 'savagery' and 'uncultured' is a theme that runs through all of the descriptions of indigenous populations. To the invading European forces, the foreign nature of ancient and traditional customs was seen as backwards and uncivilised, merely because they did not adhere to European sensibil-ities, which in turn served to distance the Western public from the inherent humanity of non-Europeans. This would pit the indigenous religious and cultural practices of much of the rest of the world at odds with the colonial Christian West, especially its outlook on sexuality.

Though initially under the purview of ecclesiastical courts, by the 1530s England had enacted the country's first civil sodomy law, the Buggery Act of 1533. Until 1861 anal penetration would remain a capital offence, with the decriminalisation of homosexual acts not coming into force until 1967. The legacy of British attitudes towards sex and gender would still be felt to this day across many of its former colonies.

> *Take up the White Man's burden*
> *The savage wars of peace*
> *Fill full the mouth of Famine*
> *And bid the sickness cease;*

'The White Man's Burden', RUDYARD KIPLING

The apparent 'burden' of white colonisers to be a civilising force in the non-Western world was a sentiment shared by many European nations. Using Christianity as a justification, Britain, Belgium, France and the Netherlands sought to homogenise and reform the 'uncivilised' African traditions and norms. Under the pretext of benevolent missions, Christianity was used as a divisive tool to erase and quell 'native practices'. The supposed 'divine right' that many Westerners felt evangelising in Africa was encapsulated in the memoir of one American monk, Daniel Kumler Flickinger, writing in the late nineteenth century. 'The only reason why our theological views are not as foolish and corrupting as theirs [Ethiopians], and that we are not believers in witchcraft, devil-worship, and a thousand other foolish things, is simply because the light of Heaven shines upon us'.

The binary that played out between believer and non-believer, Christian or devil-worshipper, would extend to everyday attire. As Christian missionaries sought to impose their oppressive norms, Flickinger would later write: 'We publicly and privately preached the gospel of dress, and showed the people that their licentious practices could never be corrected until they dressed. Nakedness is a crime against humanity, and contrary to the law of God and should be punished severely. The great curse of Africa – that which causes more converts to backslide than all other evils is licentiousness; and nakedness conduces much to it.'

Yet the contempt which colonising forces held for

African traditions and attitudes towards sexuality was not unique. As early as the 1590s, the British traveller Andrew Battell would write about his experience in Angola: 'They are beastly in their living, for they have men in women's apparel, whom they keep among their wives.'

So successful was the British criminalisation of life-styles deemed to be sinful and unchristian that, to this day, two-thirds of Commonwealth nations still criminalise homosexuality. The lasting effect of the conflation of native cultural traditions with Christian moral standards cannot be understated. In 1910, Christians made up less than 10 per cent of the population of sub-Saharan Africa. By 2010, that figure was as high as 63 per cent. The excision and replacement of indigenous practices was such that within a few generations, to many Africans, homosexuality was seen as a Western import rather than the homophobic laws of British colonisers. A study in 2016 measuring public attitudes to LGBTQ+ rights in Africa asked whether same-sex attraction was a Western phenomenon. More than half of respondents from Uganda (54 per cent) and Nigeria (51 per cent) believed it to be the case, with those asked in Ghana and Kenya polling similarly high (49 per cent and 48 per cent respectively).

The scarcity of written history on the continent has allowed this myth to propagate. What little written evidence there is, however, demonstrates that, much like the rest of the world, same-sex practices were normal and common-place in pre-colonial Africa. In the 1940s, the ethnologist Eva Meyerowitz observed that among the Ashanti and Akan in Ghana, 'men who dressed as women and engaged in homosexual relations with other men were not stigmatized, but accepted'. In positing Africa and its citizens as diametrically opposed to the civilised nature of the West, the myth was created of a singular, homogenous African identity, rather than one full of the idiosyncrasies and nuances that existed throughout an entire continent. In much the same way as the social construct of race proved helpful in classifying people of African heritage, Victorian ideas about the construct of *sexuality* proved helpful in eradicating and replacing indigenous customs and practices.

As African leaders sought to distinguish themselves from former colonial powers in the aftermath of independence, the LGBT community would be targeted as scapegoats. Robert Mugabe capitalised on anti-imperialist sentiment by constantly referring to homosexuality as the 'white man's disease', referring to the LGBT community as 'worse than dogs and pigs', while the long-time president of Uganda, Yoweri Museveni, further misrepresented the facts, declaring, 'I hear European homosexuals are recruiting in Africa. We used to have very few homosexuals traditionally.' As Museveni claimed that it is 'clear that is not how God arranged things to be', the national stance on harsher laws against LGBT communities is especially ironic given the country's history with the Christian faith and homosexuality. Between 1885 and 1887, Kabaka (King) Mwanga of Buganda, what is now central Uganda, would order the execution of twenty-two of his male pages who had recently converted to Catholicism. In accordance with their new-found religion, they had reportedly rejected Kabaka Mwanga's desire for physical intimacy. Within three years of Mwanga's deposition and subsequent exile from Buganda, homosexuality would be criminalised and the pages who Mwanga had ordered executed would be canonised as martyrs to the Catholic faith in 1920.

For many African Nationalist leaders, the persecution of LGBTQ+ communities has allowed them to present themselves as anti-colonialists, rejecting what they claim is imported 'Western culture'. Yet in today's supposedly postcolonial world, many conservative Western evangelical missionaries – under the guise of Christianity, a religion imported by colonial missions – have taken the baton of preaching homophobia across Africa. In one federal court case against the US evangelist Scott Lively, who helped promote a bill in Uganda calling for members of the LGBTQ+ community to serve life-terms in prison, the US judge was damning in his ruling: 'The question before the court is not whether the defendant's actions in aiding and abetting efforts to demonize, intimidate, and injure LGBTQ+ people in Uganda constitute violations of international law. They do.'

The vestiges of Western homophobia are living in congregations and government buildings across the continent and the African diaspora. Back home in Britain, I was all too aware what certain members of my Nigerian family might think of me if my sexuality was deemed 'un-African' and, as

I hit puberty and was beginning to define my own sexuality, I overheard the same rhetoric echoing at family gatherings.

Just as my voice began to break, I found myself relishing the company of my new best friend at my drama class. With the end of the school rugby season and my pubescent vocal chords demanding I take an enforced leave of absence from the choir for the best part of six months, suddenly my Saturday schedule had freed up. Previously, I was rushing across London, from one activity to the next. But now I had comparatively huge amounts of time to make my own way to the Anna Scher Theatre School, where I would soon develop the biggest talent crush on a fellow actor, Jimmy. Jimmy was cool. Effortlessly cool. He could sing, dance, act, and had a precocious ease on the stage that the rest of us simply marvelled at. Although he was a year older than me, outside of school that wasn't as much of a concern and, before long, we would become inseparable.

Using landline telephones, we would coordinate our departure times to ensure that we got the same bus in on a Saturday, leaving far too early to ensure we had the time to walk along Upper Street and talk gossip and nonsense. A whole innocent summer before I would be accosted near the same street by a group of teenagers attempting to rob me, we joked in each other's company in a way that felt both delicate but natural. Both of us were guilty of occasionally employing the most circuitous bus route home and breaking parental curfew for the extra minutes it granted us in each other's company. And all the while, I had just one recurring thought: Jimmy is so damn cool! Yet even as we luxuriated in the comfort of our friendship, we would engage in the 'macho ritual' of boasting about which girls in the class we had a crush on, who we thought we had a chance with and who we would make our girlfriend one day soon. The day would come very soon; sooner than I had thought, at any rate.

As the summer holidays approached, two weeks before the end of term, we were sat on the 43 bus going down the Holloway Road. Jimmy turned to me excitedly to tell me about the girl in his year at school who he had kissed just the day before and that they were boyfriend and girlfriend now. I tried to share his animation at the fact 'she don't live with her dad anymore and her mum has to work, so she's gonna have a free house all summer and I think this might be it, you know!' And it was. I would go to Ireland with my family for the majority of the summer holidays and, by the time I returned in September, it was back to my packed Saturday schedule of rugby in the morning and singing choral masses in the evening, with only a two-hour slot in the middle to fit in a drama class. Jimmy and I would stay close friends, but mock exams and finally GCSEs meant that we would never again have as much unfettered time with each other. I still thought he was damn cool. And we still got on famously. But we weren't inseparable. Nothing was ever spoken. I'm not sure if anything ever needed to be spoken. I'm not sure if I had spoken, what I might have said. I didn't even know what I felt or if it meant anything. Just that I had a very deep affection for my friend. And that that friend happened to be the same gender as me.

For Anthony, his silence was less from a certainty of his sexuality, but more from a fear of being rejected by those whom he held dearest.

'I remember the day exactly. It was Christmas and I must have been thirteen. Christmas Day. The day you've been looking forward to. Your family are there – aunties, cousins. You're pulling crackers and having a great time. The *EastEnders* Christmas special is gonna be on. And your dad is there, cutting the turkey. Seemingly out of nowhere he starts telling that story. About Sodom and Gomorrah? He's there cutting and he just goes, "There was a reason that God killed those gays. Me? I would never have a gay son. I would just never accept it. It's just ridiculous. For me," he says, pouring the gravy over his food, "it's disgusting."

'I was just thirteen. I'm there trying to eat my turkey and potatoes. And my dad has just told me he won't accept me. For something I have no control over. I remember thinking, what can I do, to not be this way? What can I read? Who can I hang out with?'

As much as the teachers at school felt hamstrung in stamping out homophobic bullying from a legal standpoint, there was also the cultural aspect of under-reporting abuse for fear of the ramifications to the home life. So when solace or friendship was offered, Anthony often felt the need to accept it on conditional grounds.

'Yeah, I actually had a really close relationship with Isaac.

But he was super alpha male, a rugby player, and I know he didn't know better but . . . so, he used to call me poofter. And like, you know you're meant to be friends, so you accept it. But that hurts, you know? Having someone who you know cares about you and has your back but still uses those words? You have to justify it in your own head. You try and reclaim it. You just want to be accepted.'

This desire for acceptance is something that many members of the LGBTQ+ community struggle with. The Albert Kennedy Trust, an organisation that supports young LGBTQ+ people aged between sixteen and twenty-five, estimates that in the UK, 150,000 were either homeless or at risk of homelessness as a result of intolerance. The study found that the main reasons were parental rejection, abuse within the family or being exposed to aggression and violence. Yet there is a distinct racialised disparity. According to a recent Stonewall study, 88 per cent of white respondents reported acceptance from within their communities. However, among Black and Asian members of the LGBTQ+ community, this number falls to below 42 per cent. The lack of support from friends and family can create a huge sense of alienation, which, according to an older West Indian actor colleague of mine, Samuel, can take years to unlearn.

'I knew that it was safer for me to pass as straight; that I would have an easier time of it straight acting. But what that did was it created a sort of disconnect between the hormones that were raging in my body and my sexual maturity; my puberty and my sexuality. I can't help but wonder if they had had happened simultaneously, would I have this disconnect between sex and intimacy? Because it's there. Especially with the rise of dating apps, which can be a mess.'

While the rejection from family and friends can be deeply hurtful, many Black LGBTQ+ people have also suffered racism from within the queer community. According to research, three in five Black LGBTQ+ people have reported experiencing discrimination or poor treatment within their local LGBTQ+ network. For many, it is a saddening but no less frustrating reality of being Black and LGBTQ+ in Britain. Both Samuel and Anthony seem stoic about the fine line between personal preference and people being crassly exclusionary. The pendulum could swing wildly from receiving opening lines to conversations asking to see their 'big Black cock' to reading bios on dating apps boldly declaring, 'No Blacks, No Fats, No Asians'. Samuel confesses to indulging past lovers in their objectification of him because he had so readily divorced sex from the intimacy of a relationship, the belief that the two were somehow separate allowing him to justify to himself the racially charged language that his lovers used to describe him. Only years later, when Samuel found himself dating a fellow Black man, would some of the complexities of interracial dating be alleviated. 'When Samson and I were seeing each other, we didn't need to talk about race. We would occasionally but it was in the context of how our families had responded to our coming out when we were growing up. We never needed to explain racism to each other. There was an ease and a comfort in that.'

For many queer People of Colour, choosing to date other queer People of Colour on dating apps is less of a preference and more of a pre-emptive strategy to protect themselves from racist abuse. In response to the protests at the murder of George Floyd, the queer dating app, Grindr would post a statement saying, 'Racism has no place in our community. To help do our part, we have decided to remove the ethnicity filter from the Grindr app. Once the filter is removed, users will no longer be able to filter profiles by ethnicity.' The move was, however, seen as tokenistic and superficial by some who believed that the company's typically slow response to the reporting of racist profiles on the app was a more pressing matter. Black writer and critic Jason Okundaye believed the choice to remove the filters was misguided. 'Grindr hasn't considered that many People of Colour, particularly those who live in majority white areas, rely on these filters to find each other. Many have absolutely no interest in interacting with white men on the app and that should be supported.'

Although much progress has been made in the struggle for equality in the LGBTQ+ community, for some the constant compromise is tiring and a concern not held by their straight counterparts, especially in the workplace.

'I've gotten used to it by now,' Samuel confides, 'the sort of backhanded compliment. The "Wait, you're gay? I would never have known. You seem so normal" that drops halfway through a rehearsal process. And I'm not trying to hide anything, but I'll be honest I admit I enjoy it because I only want to be judged for my work, not for my sexuality. I can't be bothered with the questions that come with it. Endless. And people trying to define you. I have definitely slept with women in the past, but I identify as gay. Sure it's a cliché, but yeah, it's a spectrum.'

Similarly, I recall Anthony first informing the rest of the year that he was bisexual. 'I was very much "bi now, gay later". It was safer for sure. I remember thinking that maybe if I told the rest of the year that I was still attracted to girls that it would soften the blow of me being gay. That it would be more acceptable somehow.'

His efforts would be in vain, however. Both to the rest of my year and to me, peer pressure had taught us all that confessing an attraction to the same gender was a dereliction of masculinity. In our teenage minds, we could not hold the space for a broader, 'spectral' understanding of sexuality. I would not allow it in my own mind. From the homophobic slurs that were thrown around to the querying from girl-friends of 'You're sure you're not? Because you sing a lot and you seem so comfortable around so and so . . . ' that I would begin to resent the implication. Despite all of the legal progress that has been made in the past three decades in repealing homophobic laws, attitudes do not reverse at the ratification of a law, and centuries of bigotry is not annulled by royal assent. Confronting those attitudes when espoused by some of my closest friends would prove difficult.

It would be Michaela Coel's critically acclaimed *I May Destroy You* that would really ignite the debate. The BBC/ HBO drama is an exploration of consent centring on

Arabella, a young Black woman who is sexually assaulted. As she deals with the aftermath of the incident, she is aided by her two best friends, Terry and Kwame, who throughout the series have to negotiate their own responses to sexual trauma and the murkier areas of consent. Kwame, a young Black gay man who in an earlier episode is sexually assaulted, attempts to relay to his two friends that he believes sexuality to be a spectrum and that because he doesn't feel safe being intimate with a man, he will attempt a date with a woman. Arabella laughs at the idea, declaring that, 'I'm not straight, I just love dick.'

Kwame then takes a video call from a white girl called Nilufer, organising a date with her later on. The date having gone well, Kwame accompanies Nilufer, who giggles while confessing what her 'type' is. 'I'm into guys with some edge. I'm into Black guys? Could you tell? I'm really into Black guys.' Despite the obvious fetishisation, the pair start having sex, with Nilufer's assertiveness pushing Kwame past his hesitancy. The act however is triggering for Kwame, bringing flashbacks of his assault as Nilufer urges him on. Enjoying a post-coital spliff, the pair begin rapping along to a song on the radio, wherein Nilufer substitutes the N-word with 'Nijja', justifying herself in the face of Kwame's mockery that 'I've got a lot of Black friends. I would never say it ... It's complex, isn't it?' She does however feel comfortable using the word 'faggot', and laughs at Kwame calling it the F-word, pointing to not having 'much sympathy with major appropriators of the female identity'. When Kwame confides in her that he is gay and wanted to experiment with 'the spectrum', she is enraged, calling him a 'fucking dick' and ridiculing the fact that he was a virgin. Later, his best friend Arabella is infuriated to find out about his sexual encounter, accusing Kwame of having sex with Nilufer under false pretences. As Kwame tries to protest, claiming Nilufer effectively 'forced' him to have sex with her, she rebuffs his attempt at claiming victimhood, asserting that 'being vulnerable doesn't mean you can make other people vulnerable, doesn't mean you can put other people through pain'. This sat uncomfortably with me in the most honest sense, as it was an accurate portrayal of the binary way in which male sexuality and especially Black male sexuality is often viewed.

The belief that Kwame had sex with Nilufer 'under false pretences' was one shared by two Black female friends of mine. 'Nah, he was wrong, man. Listen, if I ever found out that my man had even kissed another man, even if it was just messing around in a game of spin the bottle or playing around at uni, that would be it. If that's what you're trying to do with the next man, then why are you with me?' When I queried what difference it made if you were in a monogamous relationship, my other friend chimed in, 'Because I can't give you that. If you want to be with a man, then be with one. I want a real Black man that can hold me down and feel safe in our relationship, not worrying or insecure they'll run off.' Hearing this bi-phobic language from close friends, I repeatedly tried to counter it, but before long, I would hear a familiar phrase: 'What does it matter, Obi? It's just a personal preference.' I could sense my friends' patience wearing thin. The matter seems, as Nilufer put it, complex. Yet simultaneously is simple.

The writer and civil rights activist Audre Lorde wrote the following in an essay entitled 'There is No Hierarchy of Oppressions'.

'Any attack against Black people is a lesbian and gay issue, because I and thousands of other Black women are part of the lesbian community. Any attack against lesbians and gays is a Black issue, because thousands of lesbians and gay men are Black. There is no hierarchy of oppression.

'I cannot afford the luxury of fighting one form of oppression only. I cannot afford to believe that freedom from intolerance is the right of only one particular group. And I cannot afford to choose between the fronts upon which I must battle these forces of discrimination, wherever they appear to destroy me. And when they appear to destroy me, it will not be long before they appear to destroy you.'

Despite my parents' best attempts to immerse me in both Irish and Nigerian culture, the ease of trips to Ireland compared to Nigeria meant that by the time I was old enough, I felt somewhat disconnected from my heritage on my father's side. The lack of interest I had shown in learning the Igbo language was something that I sought to put right now that I was an adult. It was to this purpose that I joined a WhatsApp group filled with native Igbo speakers who were living in Britain. Many of them had lived here for many years, but I was one of the youngest in the group. The cultural norms meant that I was constantly deferring to my elders and often biting my tongue when comments I regarded as culturally insensitive were raised.

On one of the more active days of conversation in the group, I returned to my phone to find more than one hundred messages. Onyinyechi, a fellow second-generation Nigerian woman, had stated, 'We cannot say Black Lives Matter until All Black Lives Matter. That means Women, LGBTQ+, Disabled. EVERYONE.' As I read through the messages, I was appalled as, one by one, elders who had had jovial to and fro about Nigeria and the diaspora – full of support for one another and boasting of praiseworthy accomplishments both in London and at home – began to chastise and castigate Onyinyechi. Some chose to quote from Leviticus, while others took umbrage with her tone. Claims of 'sinful behaviour that we don't have at home' were typed in capital letters, while others would protest 'today homosexuality; tomorrow paedophilia!' All the while Onyinyechi tried to maintain a sense of decorum and respect. By the time I had finally caught up with all the messages, my patience had eroded to the point where I could not entertain such civility.

It wasn't the first time I'd come across such false equivalences, nor was it a specifically Nigerian issue. But hearing these words from members of my own community, no matter how distantly related they were, was exasperating. I lost my temper. Beyond the inherent intolerance they were displaying, my thoughts raged with the knowledge that I was an older brother and had just recently become an uncle. I couldn't shift the thought that by staying silent I would be portraying Onyinyechi as some rogue outlier, a radical intent on disregarding her heritage and customs when all she was asking for was for us to be more inclusive in our thoughts, actions and activism. My silence in that instance would be a violent, tacit approval of the group mentality that was being used to cudgel and chastise Onyinyechi as a rod of correction. As respectful as I wanted to be to my culture, I would not accept this limited view of what it meant to be a 'Good Respectful Nigerian Man', especially when so much of that tradition was rooted in a culture that was not my own.

The aftermath of the discussion was not pretty. Several times, older members demanded that the group administrator remove both Onyinyechi and me from the group. An uneasy peace was reached when it was agreed that 'contentious issues' would not be discussed on the forum, as we would all respect each other's religious and cultural beliefs. As the dust settled, I ruminated on whether any minds had been changed or rather, had we all become more entrenched, staunchly defending our positions? For many people their spiritual beliefs, be they religious, agnostic or atheistic, are deeply personal parts of their identity. The marrying of it with cultural identity in a society that can often be demeaning on a personal level has proven to be difficult to navigate.

More than a decade and a half after Jimmy became my best friend, my mind drifted back to the intense summer we spent together. As a teen I identified as straight, owing to the fact that I never found myself physically attracted to another man. My intense friendship with Jimmy was justified in both my teenage and later adult mind as just a 'talent crush'. Nevertheless, a burning question began to weigh on my mind as I felt the reverberations of my argument within my Igbo language group continue.

Dad was alone in the kitchen making a cup of tea when I plucked up the courage to ask him, 'If any of us, any of the boys had come out to you and Mum, or brought home a boyfriend, would that have been allowed? I mean would you . . . ' I trailed off. My dad fixed me with his kindly eyes and simply said, 'It would have been perfectly normal.'

Black history, despite having a month dedicated to it since 1987 in the UK, is still suffering the aftermath of the evisceration of many cultural practices by the British Empire and other colonial forces. The consequence of this has led to an awkward reckoning with what it means to be anti-colonial but still culturally connected to African heritage. Challenging the anti-LGBTQ+ legislation in Uganda, David Cameron threatened to withdraw aid to the country, as they 'were not adhering to proper human rights'. This drew the response from one presidential adviser: 'But this kind of ex-colonial mentality of saying, "You do this or I withdraw my aid" will definitely make people extremely uncomfortable with being treated like children.' This charged dynamic between a nation that has historically been responsible for the enforced cultural amnesia, violent purging and supplanting of indigenous religion and tradition and its former colonies plays out on both the political and the personal level.

Ultimately, I'm glad that Cameron reversed his anti-LGBTQ+ stance of previous years with the belated passing of the Marriage (Same Sex Couples) Act which introduced civil marriage for same-sex couples in England and Wales in 2013 and used Britain's international pressure to call for equality and equal rights. But the challenge that is ahead of us demands education, compassion and patience, not only for those who have been and still are affected by the oppressive laws and mindsets that Britain is in large part responsible for, but for those who will come after us. The world and Britain's place in it, is changing. We can ill-afford to be left behind.

7

Proper British

> *A study by the Migration Observatory at the*
> *University of Oxford in 2013 said that the*
> *proportion of minority groups living in Britain*
> *will rise to 40 per cent by 2050 and that if current*
> *trends continue the so-called majority-ethnic*
> *group in the UK – white British – will be a*
> *minority before 2070.*

It was during a robust conversation on the panel discussion show *The Pledge* between LBC presenter Nick Ferrari and author and journalist Afua Hirsch discussing historical figures and how they should be celebrated that Ferrari would repeat sentiments that echoed the conditionality that many Black Britons feel underlines their experience in this country. Raised in Wimbledon to an English father and a Ghanaian mother, Hirsch has long advocated for Britain to revaluate the narrative of its past and question whether the history that children are taught in schools helps to entrench divides in society rather than heal them. This call for a more robust debate has often put her at loggerheads with some more conservative commentators, not least some of her fellow panellists on *The Pledge*. When Hirsch posited whether historical figures like Cecil Rhodes and Winston Churchill's legacies should be interrogated, Ferrari made a leap into personal attack that was as offensive as it was unsurprising.

'Why do you stay in this country, if you take such offence when you see Nelson's Column, if you take such offence when you hear Winston Churchill's name? I would argue in the unlikely event that anybody wanted to have a poll, probably eighty to ninety per cent of people would say Winston Churchill did a good thing. I'm delighted that I see you each Thursday . . . but if it offends you so much, how do you manage to stay here?'

Despite being a British citizen, the suggestion that, merely because her mother is of Ghanaian heritage, Hirsch is apparently precluded from critiquing British historical figures is not a rarity. As uncomfortable as it is to acknowledge, Ferrari's implication is firmly rooted in Hirsch's heritage; that it somehow makes her critiques less valid or that she is somehow less British. As Hirsch defended herself – 'The reason I raise this critique is not because I hate Britain, it's because I care about this country'– I thought how rarely white Britons are told that they can leave the country if they disapprove of the direction the country is going in.

My own experiences of being told to 'go back home' have been plentiful enough throughout the years. However, watching this clip, it was one of the most recent occurrences that came to mind, happening as it did two days after the Brexit referendum. The abuse, hurled from a passing van, almost made me laugh in its absurdity: 'Go back to Cuba, you bloody immigrant.' Obviously I had underestimated the depth of anti-Cuban sentiment in London. But there was no doubt my outward appearance had invited racist abuse.

This ever-present xenophobic attitude, which still permeates much of British society, makes it difficult to view the changing demographic of Britain as 'the antidote for racism' without a degree of scepticism. Fears about the changing makeup of British society have been stoked by many in power throughout the country's history, with one of the more pithy criticisms of self-professed patriots coming from Samuel Johnson in his 1774 pamphlet *The Patriot*. 'Patriotism is the last refuge of the scoundrel.'

My being born and raised in this country could not shield me from the xenophobic sentiments that had led to my racist abuse, which had been stoked by certain sections of the media. How could I expect it to, if not even members of the royal family were protected from the racist focus of the media?

When Prince Harry and Meghan Markle wed in 2018, it was heralded in many quarters as a watermark moment for Britain, the equivalent of Obama being elected President of the United States in 2008. Having been seen by many younger Brits as an old-fashioned institution linked with colonialism and an era often seen through rose-tinted glasses, for some Britain's royal family did not represent the modern face of Britain. In 2000, Lady Gavron, the vice-chairwoman of a commission for the Runnymede Trust, Britain's leading independent race equality think tank, would scandalise the nation by suggesting the political capital that could be gained by a royal interracial marriage for Prince Charles: 'It would have been great if Prince Charles had been told to marry someone Black. Imagine what message that would have sent out.'

Fewer than two decades later and his son would fall in love with and marry Meghan Markle, a woman whose mother was African-American. Some media outlets, however, would take issue with Harry's choice of romantic partner. The *Spectator* commented, 'Obviously, 70 years ago, Meghan Markle would have been the kind of woman the Prince would have had for a mistress, not a wife.' The *Daily Mail*, meanwhile, would run with the headline, 'Harry's girl is (almost) straight outta Compton', attempting to link Meghan to the pervasive anti-Black narratives that have long populated both British and US media.

The media focus became so intense that seventy-two female Members of Parliament wrote a letter of solidarity to Markle over what they called 'outdated, colonial undertones'. Prince Harry would also make a statement criticising 'the racial undertones of comment pieces' and the 'outright sexism and racism of social media trolls and web article comments'. Despite the very privileged position the pair of them held, Markle's heritage and background appeared to make her fair game for those who sought to express racist ideas. Many in the media would have to engage in editorial gymnastics in order to downplay and reframe their criticism and snarky comments about the couple, but perhaps the most unseemly and blatant racially loaded moment of the young couple's life was the targeting of their days-old child, moments after he had left the hospital.

As the world got their first glimpse of the new royal baby, Archie Harrison, broadcaster Danny Baker, in a now-deleted tweet, captioned a picture of a couple holding hands with a monkey dressed in a suit: 'Royal baby leaves hospital'. The subsequent media storm and retribution was swift and, shortly after, Baker was fired by the BBC. Although only days old, baby Archie had found himself drawn into a media furore with his crime simply being born to a mixed-race woman. Even if we were to give Baker the benefit of the doubt, that he simply posted a tweet about a monkey in a suit which he had employed to 'lampoon privilege', this country has a long and colourful history of comparing people with African ancestry to apes. Monkey chants and the throwing of banana skins are endemic in football, a sport that Baker follows religiously, and yet somehow he did not recognise how this could cause offence.

Even before he had been born, Archie would be exoticised, with Rachel Johnson extolling his ability to 'thicken [the royal family's] watery, thin blue blood and Spencer pale skin and ginger hair with some rich and exotic DNA'. This rhetoric, however, was taken further by the former head of the Equality and Human Rights Commission, Trevor Phillips. In a surreal move, Phillips would pen an open letter to the newborn, informing the child that he would have to bear 'some responsibility to be a bridge between white Britain and Black Britain on your shoulders. Everyone will be watching to see how you manage being the inheritor of two very different traditions.' For many, however, this rose-tinted outlook that interracial relationships would be the magic bullet against racism was not exceptional and very much represented their worldview.

Shortly after the murder of George Floyd, there were several protests in central London attended by people of all races, ages and genders chanting and carrying placards in solidarity with the Black community. As the march progressed, one sign, carried by a white woman caught my eye. It read: 'Stop Shooting Black Men. I Want To Have Brown Babies.'

Much like the 'personal preference' stated by my friends, I was struck by the problematic nature of this statement. For many people, their proximity to either Black lovers or children gives an impression of personal immunity from criticism regarding the thorny issue of race. Indeed, this was the defence of former Olympian Sharron Davies when critiqued online for comparing drag to Blackface, tweeting: 'With mixed race kids & loads of wonderful friends from all over the world I don't think I can be accused of racism.'

Reading Davies's tweet, I could not help but be acutely aware of the way in which her children had been reduced to props that somehow implied her lack of complicity, consciously or not, in a society that still had very far to go in countering centuries of racist narratives and the privileging of people from certain backgrounds. Having spent the majority of my adult life cognisant of the anti-Black narratives that I had internalised, I was ill at ease with the assumption that having and raising a child in an interracial relationship granted parents immunity from the necessary work of anti-racism. Although the child of one myself, and to this day grateful that my parents raised me in an environment in which I was constantly surrounded by and engaged with my Nigerian heritage, the sexist and racist water of British culture in which I was swimming growing up meant that it was a constant battle not to imbibe some of those same ideas, regardless of my parentage.

One need only look to the US to recognise that children of mixed heritage are not the panacea for racism. Black women who were enslaved were for centuries consistently subjected to sexual violence, rape and forced reproduction by white men. It is broadly agreed by historians that Thomas Jefferson, for instance, one of the US's Founding Fathers and its third president, would go on to rape his slave Sally Hemmings, and that she would have at least six children by him. This is the author of the phrase, 'We hold these truths to be sacred & undeniable; that all men are created equal & independent' in the Declaration of Independence.

Whatever familial link Jefferson felt towards his descendants, many of whom are alive today, was not enough to prick his conscience into attempting to abolish slavery. Rather, the children of mixed heritage from these relationships would later be deemed Black by the 'one-drop rule', which asserted that 'every person who shall have one-eighth or more of negro blood shall be deemed and held to be a person of color'. Being designated as a 'person of colour', or more specifically *not white*, was essential in the upholding of segregationist policies and white supremacy.

The awkward truth is that if sex was enough to save us from the spectre of racism, it would have done so by now, especially in a country as ethnically diverse as the US. Having mixed-race children can be a person's first awakening to the issues many Black people face. This was apparently the case with Kim Kardashian who, after having a daughter called North with the rapper Kanye West, would discover that racism still existed. 'To be honest, before I had North, I never really gave racism or discrimination a lot of thought. It is obviously a topic that Kanye is passionate about, but I guess it was easier for me to believe that it was someone else's battle. But recently, I've read and personally experienced some incidents that have sickened me and made me take notice. I realize that racism and discrimination are still alive, and just as hateful and deadly as they ever have been.'

Individual children of mixed heritage cannot be expected to single-handedly dismantle white supremacy, especially when raised by parents whose ability to acknowledge Black people's humanity is only catalysed by realising that their own child will be victim to such prejudices. Current trends project that Britain will become more ethnically diverse and that our attitudes towards race, and the language we use to discuss it, will need to evolve. The British government, however, has not only shown a reluctance to do this; it has doubled down by showing a willingness to contravene international law to render British subjects stateless – as in the case of Shamima Begum.

Shamima Begum was born a British citizen under UK law. Until the age of fifteen, she attended school at the Bethnal Green Academy in London. It was at that age that in February of 2015 she would fly from Gatwick to Istanbul with two of her classmates. It would later transpire that the teenager had been groomed and radicalised online. She made her way from Turkey to Syria to join IS and, ten days after arriving in Syria, was married to Dutch-born Yago Riedijk, with whom she would go on to have three children. It was while she was pregnant with the third of these children that she was found by *The Times* war correspondent Anthony Loyd in a refugee camp in Northern Syria. Five days later, Begum would be interviewed by the BBC where she would go on to state her desire to return to Britain. Home Secretary Sajid Javid would later announce that an order had been made to strip Begum of her British citizenship and declared that she would never be allowed back into the country. This was a direct contradiction to his predecessor Theresa May, who stated in 2014 that the UK will not remove citizenship from IS fighters born in the UK as 'it is illegal for any country to make its citizens stateless'.

Presumably this position was forgotten three years later when May was the serving prime minister. The UK government would contend that Begum had or was entitled to Bangladeshi citizenship, despite this being denied by the Bangladeshi government who, operating under a zero-tolerance policy for terrorism, publicly stated that Begum would face the death penalty were she to enter the country. Both UN international law (1961 Convention on the Reduction of Statelessness), of which the UK is a signatory, and UK National law (British Nationality Act 1981) make it illegal to render a citizen stateless, a fact that Javid would have certainly been made aware of by the Home Office.

Between 2018 and 2019, more than 18,000 children were suspected of being victims of child exploitation, with campaigners saying that the true figure is far higher. After Begum arrived in Syria, she was called 'jihadi' or 'IS bride'. Yet, as unpalatable as it may be for us to accept, the radicalisation that Begum underwent happened in Britain. She was targeted and groomed online and was failed by those who were charged to protect her. While her actions may seem irredeemable and unfathomable to the majority of the British public, we cannot indemnify ourselves against the failure to protect her from adults who sought to target her no matter how politically expedient it might be.

Javid was slammed by human rights campaigners not only for trying to engage in an action that violated international law, but also for failing to acknowledge that Begum was the victim of abuse. Hiding behind the defence that, because of her Bangladeshi heritage, Britain was absolved of responsibility implies that there is still a two-tier citizenship to which Begum is subject. By no means are Begum's actions defensible, and her disgraceful statements to the press have been uncomfortable to digest. Under a headline 'Shamima Begum: six shocking quotes that will send shivers down your spine', the *Daily Express* quoted Begum's response to IS executions: 'Yeah, I knew about those things and I was okay with it. Because, you know, I started becoming religious just before I left. From what I heard, Islamically that is all allowed. So I was okay with it.' By her own admission, she was a child when her journey to radicalisation began. Yet this fact is often overlooked by a British press and government who seem reticent to accept that she has been groomed.

But had her parents and grandparents been white and born in Britain, her treatment by the government would have been different as she would have had no other country to be passed off to. Bangladesh is a country that Begum has never visited, nor claimed citizenship in, so to demand they take responsibility for her is an abdication by the very government that failed her.

In the aftermath of the London Bridge terror attack of 2017, Theresa May addressed the nation with a speech that sought to highlight the inability of terrorists to undermine British unity and plurality.

'They are bound together by the single, evil ideology of Islamist extremism that preaches hatred, sows division, and promotes sectarianism. It is an ideology that claims our Western values of freedom, democracy and human rights are incompatible with the religion of Islam. It is an ideology that is a perversion of Islam and a perversion of the truth. Defeating this ideology is one of the great challenges of our time. But it cannot be defeated through military intervention alone ... It will only be defeated when we turn people's minds away from this violence and make them understand that our values – pluralistic, British values – are superior to anything offered by the preachers and supporters of hate.'

May is correct in her assertion that one of the best ways to defeat those who would seek to promote division is to show our commitment to values of inclusivity and pluralism. The challenge then for the British government in negotiating its changing demographics is how it chooses to address its citizens. As offensive as Nick Ferrari's comments to Afua Hirsch were, they are mirrored by the domestic policy that maintains that 'British nationality is a privilege and the Home Secretary has the ability to remove it from dual nationals when she believes it to be in the public good.' The comfort that I felt listening to Theresa May's words after a time of national tragedy suddenly felt distinctly undercut by knowing that my citizenship could be under threat if it was deemed to be in the public interest. How committed is

Britain to human rights if it is willing to violate international law to strip its own citizens of statehood? Just like Hirsch, I care very much about my country. Occasionally, however, it feels like Britain does not reciprocate those feelings.

The anxiety over having British citizens who hail from certain parts of the world is nothing new. One of the most famous examples of questioning the loyalty of British citizens was coined after the Conservative politician Norman Tebbit suggested in an interview in 1990 that immigrants to Britain were failing to integrate properly, stating: 'A large proportion of Britain's Asian population fail to pass the cricket test. Which side do they cheer for? It's an interesting test. Are you still harking back to where you came from or where you are?'

The 'cricket test' or 'Tebbit test' would be discussed, referenced and argued over for many months after Tebbit's comments to criticise the lack of integration of immigrants from the West Indies and south Asia. Curiously, this standard is never applied to football fans during the European Championships, or indeed to rugby fans in World Cup tournaments. This demand for fealty to English sporting teams does not extend to immigrants from Australasia or North America, or indeed to the rest of Europe; even the terminology applied to immigrants from those countries is sanitised to *expatriates*. Modern-day politicians have long since retired the use of the dog-whistle racial language used by Tebbit and, by 2012, Nick Clegg, the deputy prime minister at the time, would boldly state, 'I'm not sure if my children who were wearing their Spanish football kit, given to them by Miriam, would have passed the Norman Tebbit cricket test.'

Nonetheless, the sentiment is still present in the micro-aggressions that occur when meeting somebody for the first time and 'the question' comes. It is one that most People of Colour have had at some point in their lives, and whether it is born out of genuine curiosity or is a spiteful attempt to other, intent does not always trump impact. As you are asked the question, 'Where are you from?' and the response of 'I grew up in Holloway' does not sate the inquisitor's appetite, you hear your internal monologue go into overdrive. The repetition of the question in its modi-fied form, usually some variation of 'No, but where are you *from* from?', consciously or not shares spiritual kinship to Ferrari's criticism, to Tebbit's question, to Javid's citizen-ship stripping. Plurality and inclusiveness, those values that May asserted were at the heart of British society, find their foundations jeopardised by this tiering of the British identity. The lack of appetite in acknowledging these issues risks relationships of all kind: platonic, familial and even romantic.

Discussing the concept of whiteness, Noel Ignatiev, author of *How the Irish Became White* wrote, 'The members go through life accepting the benefits of membership with-out thinking about the cost.' Much like Kim Kardashian, some people do not confront the issue of race until they are dealing with their own children. The rude awakening that I would be subject to would leave a fissure in a friendship that would take years to heal.

I was privileged to be asked to be godfather to a close friend's daughter. On one of our trips to the park, when she was six years old, my goddaughter and I intended to test drive the new bike she had just been given for her birthday. With my goddaughter kitted out in helmet and kneepads, we spent the next hour laughing, falling, failing and occasionally succeeding to help her gain the beginnings of independence on her bike. Having not had kids yet, it felt like a privilege to help teach a child to ride a bike, a skill I would not learn until embarrassingly late into my teens.

After we had all had dinner and my friend put his daughter to bed, we sat in his living room enjoying a cold beer. After some banter about the atrocious football results Arsenal had been churning out, and thanking me for taking his daughter to the park, I detected an uncertain look on his face.

'So, Mum rang while the pair of you were out.'

'Oh, no way. Sorry to have missed her. How's she doing? How's the house in Wales?'

'Yeah, it's good. All done up now. She was bummed to miss her granddaughter.'

And then I detected that wary smile again.

'She's doing so well on the bike.'

He paused, weighing up whether he should verbalise his

217

thoughts. 'Thanks again for doing that ... so random. My mum was like, "How could you let Obi take her out to the park?" And I was like, "Why wouldn't I, Mum? They get on like a house on fire." And she was like, "Well, because someone might have called the police."'

'I ... she said what?'

'I know, right. And I was like, "But Mum, why would anyone call the police?" And she was like, "Well, because he's obviously not her father." And I just didn't know what to say. So I just kinda laughed it off. That's crazy, right?'

'I ... yeah, man. That's nuts. So ... so that's all you said to her?'

'Yeah, I mean, what else was I supposed to say?'

'No, yeah ... I just ... yeah.'

I couldn't explain it. My brain-to-tongue connection was failing me as I sought to distil in a sentence the hurt, anger and disappointment I was feeling. I grappled with it in my mind and felt my physical temperature rise as I was sat across from one of my dearest friends who, by this point, had moved on to reckoning what Arsenal's top-four chances were this year. I had met his mum. We'd even holidayed at her house in Wales and spent countless late nights socialising and playing games together at family gatherings.

He's obviously not her father.

The phenotype, or outward appearance, of any human being is superficially linked to DNA. Being of dual heritage can often mean that predicting what a child might look like (a fool's errand in any case due to the wonderful randomness of the human genome and the brilliant variations that can occur) is even more of a challenge. Nonetheless, as I considered my niece and nephew and their relatively fair outward appearance, my mind turned to my white friend sat across from me drivelling on about sports. As I thought about his mother, my heart began to sink as I realised that the reason she thought that somebody else might call the police is because she believed that was a reasonable course of action to enter into if you were to see a Black man teaching a blonde six-year-old with blue eyes how to ride a bike. The connection I had to my goddaughter did not matter; I felt the memories of our laughter curdle, tainted by her grandmother's words. My relationship to my friend's mother did not count; it wasn't me that she was concerned about, or who should be apprehended by the police – it was those 'other dangerous Black men'. Nevertheless, my friend kept blathering on about football, bemoaning the lack of Arsenal's transfer ambition, as all the while my temperature rose, and I felt the chasm between us growing.

'You should have said something,' I blurted.

'Huh?'

'To your mum. That's fucked up, man. You should have said something.'

'I did. I said she was being ridiculous and just kinda laughed it off.'

'Yeah but,' I seethed. 'It's more than ridiculous. It's . . . '

'Look, Obi. It's not that deep.'

'It's not?'

'No, man. Like, just chill out. Grab another beer and we'll catch *Match of The Day* starting in a few minutes.'

'Nah, don't worry, man. I think I'm just gonna head out.'

'It's late. You sure?'

It was. And I was certain. As the slow recognition that this wasn't a safe space for me became fully realised when I felt the sadness metastasizing through my body. If I could not rely on my best friends to call out racist language about me, no matter how indirectly, could I truly rely on them? Perhaps I was wrong to demand more from him. Perhaps it was wrong to hope that his mother should know how laced with racism her instinct was, her 'natural response' of calling the police upon seeing a Black man and a white child playing in the park together. As a white person who was rarely confronted with the issue of race, what more could I expect from him in that moment when faced with confronting his sole surviving parent on my behalf? She could have been my own child. She could have been my adopted child. She could have been precisely what she was – a family friend I was taking care of. All of these scenarios are normal, common and entirely unworthy of police attention – and to think it 'an instinct' to call 999 because I was her 'suspected kidnapper' is racist.

As disappointed as I felt on a personal level, and as let down as I was by my friend, some of the most difficult challenges I have come up against in negotiating my place as a Briton of dual heritage have been in the workplace; namely the theatres that I've had the privilege to work in.

In 1989, anti-racist activist Peggy McIntosh's essay 'White Privilege: Unpacking the Invisible Knapsack' was published. In the essay she wrote: 'I was taught to see racism only in individual acts of meanness, not in invisible systems conferring dominance on my group.' She would go on to give a list of fifty examples in her daily life that showcased the unearned privilege that she, as a white woman, was the beneficiary of, comparing it to 'an invisible weightless knapsack of special provisions, assurances, tools, maps, guides, codebooks, passports, visas, clothes, compass, emergency gear, and blank checks'. A brief selection of the examples includes the following:

- I can easily buy posters, post-cards, picture books, greeting cards, dolls, toys and children's magazines featuring people of my race.
- I can choose blemish cover or bandages in 'flesh' colour and have them more or less match my skin.
- I can go into a music shop and count on finding the music of my race represented, into a supermarket and find the staple foods which fit with my cultural traditions, into a hairdresser's shop and find someone who can cut my hair.
- My culture gives me little fear about ignoring the perspectives and powers of people of other races.
- I can criticize our government and talk about how much I fear its policies and behaviour without being seen as a cultural outsider.

Having had the chance to work on some of the more inclusive shows to have graced the West End in the past few years, from *Motown: The Musical* to *Hamilton* and even Disney's *Frozen*, I have shared the stage with some of the brightest theatrical talents in London. But it would soon become apparent that diverse casting alone is not the cure-all for the problem of years of under-representation of marginalised groups in British theatre, nor does it automatically evangelise those who work within the industry to recognising there is still work to be done.

Celebrating at Christmas drinks, my castmates and I were discussing how rare it was to be in such an inclusive show and the power that had for those in the audience. The conversation would come to an abrupt halt, however, when a white member of the production team came over and, after eavesdropping on the conversation for thirty seconds, audibly yawned and declared, 'Oh God. Are we really still talking about diversity?'

Despite appearing in three original London casts of West End musicals, and despite my choirboy background, as an aspiring actor, I did not believe that musicals were in my future. Of the few shows that I saw advertised or had the good fortune to go and see, very few of them seemed to have Black casts, with the notable exception of *The Lion King*. Though the show has stood the test of time and manages to capture audiences year after year, I could not visualise myself in the show. But when I received the call from my agent that I would be performing the role of George

Washington in *Hamilton: An American Musical,* my mind was awash with the potential for what this show could mean to those children in the audience who would look up and see a mirror; they would see a potential future for themselves represented in the characters on the stage. I would not be playing a servant or a slave or a butler but a president; the First President. For me and for many of the other actors in the *Hamilton* company, there was an acute awareness that talent and hard work was only a part of our journey to the stage. No matter how gifted we were, our success was reliant on somebody in our creative journey lifting us onto their shoulders and helping us to climb the ladder.

My awareness of the good fortune that I was blessed with in being uplifted was accentuated by the sense of loneliness I'd felt when looking at cast after cast of all-white characters in the plays, TV shows and movies I had watched my whole life. Despite all of that, I was now playing *the* Founding Father of the United States of America and audiences of all ages, colours and beliefs would be able to witness that for eight shows a week. My casting in this role would allow me to pass that ladder back down and uplift a child that, until that point, believed theatre was not for them. But the reality threatened to be different.

The demand for tickets for *Hamilton* was extremely high, with audiences having purchased tickets in some cases eighteen months in advance. The high demand for the show was deeply gratifying to experience, as we played to packed house after packed house, but the reality of commercial theatre meant that some of the tickets would cost hundreds of pounds. Being an American show, the producers had not yet determined what the outreach programme might look like. So, despite the commercial success and critical acclaim, I found myself burdened with the troubling weight of who this show was for. This bold, genre-fusing production, telling the story of the founding of the contemporary United States, with a cast of men and women from all backgrounds, that spoke to the inclusive, pluralistic best of who we could hope to be as a society was being told to an audience that was predominantly white. In the spirit of that age-old axiom, 'You have to see it to be it', I couldn't help but notice that those who did not normally see themselves represented on stage or in musicals were not being invited to see our performance. The creative team were rightfully lauded for casting a show with a diverse group of actors but our work could not stop there. There was no mention in the narrative of the near genocide of indigenous peoples, and only a passing mention of slavery, the two great stains in the country's history. Were we just presenting a sanitised, palatably contemporary version of this history of the US about rich white people, for rich white people, with a cast of predominantly Black and brown faces?

Over the course of our inaugural year at the Victoria Palace, the original cast would pull together and, with the support of the producers and especially the show's director Thomas Kail, visit schools and lead Q&A sessions with young students from London schools who might not otherwise have had the funds to watch the show. It was our small way of 'passing the ladder back down', motivated by the obstacles that each of us had had to face in our journeys to becoming actors, especially those of us who came from Black or Asian backgrounds.

'Legacy. What is a legacy? It's planting seeds in a garden you never get to see.'

This line appears in the penultimate song of the show, as Hamilton considers whether he has done enough with his life to safeguard the future of those who come after him. As satisfying as it was to go out and meet schoolchildren without access to premium theatre tickets, the cast were anxious to facilitate a schools performance. The likelihood of this happening had seemed ever decreasing, with some of the British producers attempting to temper our optimism due to logistical constraints and many of the original company leaving after their year-long contract ended. But five weeks before the end of the run, strings were pulled as Kail and the show's American producers, recognising the depth of feeling for the initiative within the cast, lent their support.

In a huge effort, schools were gathered together from all over London to come to Victoria for an extra schools performance. Of the four hundred performances of that show in front of critics, family and royalty, that schools performance will be the one that lives longest in my memory. During the opening number, the entire cast lines up at the front of the stage and looks out into the audience. And for the first time I saw an audience that looked like the London I had lived in and grown up in: young, diverse and engaged. The same young Black, white and Asian children who I had run workshops with stared up at me from the front row. I saw young Black girls listen to Walthamstow-born Rachel John's soaring vocals as Angelica Schuyler with amazement, and heard Black boys cheer Tottenham-born Tarinn Callender as he burst onto the stage as Hercules Mulligan. In this deeply American tale, it all felt proper British.

This is why such comments as 'Are we still talking about diversity?' get my hackles up. The story of Britain has and will always be 'diverse'. The question is will we choose to be inclusive. Just because a chef has only decided to use certain ingredients to prepare the same dish repeatedly does not mean that there aren't more interesting ingredients that would taste great too. Many of my white actor friends who had failed to secure a part would be informed after an audition by their agent and latterly go on to inform me that, 'they decided they wanted to go for the diversity casting'. Agents who mislead their clients like this do them a disservice by implying that it is somehow a binary equation of talented or diverse, reinforcing the narrative that non-white performers do not belong in British theatre. For those in the industry who had been shielded from the complexities of race, unaware that they had been racialised as white, or were indeed carrying an 'invisible knapsack', the choice by creatives to be more inclusive can be critiqued as oppressive to white people. This was the viewpoint of one agent who posted in a private group on Facebook: 'I'm bored of breakdowns asking for BAME actors. Casting them because of the colour of their skin because it adds that *va va voom* to the cast list, or their skills in performance? And now I see a breakdown for BAME only that *are* actor/musos [actor musicians]. It's putting talented 'white' performers out of work. I think it stinks.'

Actors, while being the most prominent members of the industry, are very rarely the decision makers. While there are still decision makers such as agents, directors, casting directors and producers who have not challenged or interrogated their racist attitudes, then, much like the persistent stain of racist abuse from football fans despite the high percentage of professional footballers of African heritage, the problem will linger on. Whether it's pitch-black underwear offered to Black performers as 'nude underwear' or a hair stylist who doesn't know how to navigate Afro hair, these microaggressions send out the message that theatre as a professional workplace is built for white people. Black performers are then faced with the dilemma of either accepting the thoughtless costume choices and unsuitable hair stylings or speaking out against them. If they do the latter, they do so knowing that many in the industry believe they are 'putting talented white performers out of work' when literally all they're asking for is equality. So, while I was blessed at *Hamilton* to be empowered by both my director and the producers to feel like I could speak out and have a voice and that it would not adversely affect my career, this has not always been the case.

Midway through my run of *The Physicists* at the Donmar Warehouse, shortly after graduating, I was told by my agent that I was successful in my audition for the winter season of plays at the main house of the Royal Shakespeare Company. Alongside three fellow graduates, I had been cast in a minor role and would understudy some of the more senior actors in the company. My parents had once driven my brothers and me to Shakespeare's home in Stratford-upon-Avon when we were children to watch an afternoon matinee. The pride on my parents' faces as they watched me perform in the Royal Shakespeare Theatre for the first time was worth more than the prestige of performing any particular role. Some actors spend years auditioning to be a part of the reputable, nationally funded company, a fact that an older actor in the company who was also making his debut at the theatre did not fail to make known to me. As I stood after a long rehearsal in the local pub, The Dirty Duck, I made the mistake of bemoaning the arduous nature of the dress rehearsal that day. It was at this point that the older actor turned to me and said, 'You should stop whining. There are plenty more talented *white* actors who would be grateful just to be here and weren't hired just because of the way they look.'

I was too hurt to be angry, chastened as I had been for being uppity. Other than an actor in his thirties, Ansu Kabia, the only other non-white actor in the company was Paapa Essiedu, another fellow graduate. I looked around to see if anybody else might have overheard the older actor's comment and realised we were alone. Beyond any inse-curity, I, like many creatives, harboured about whether I was talented enough, there was a deep assumption that my heritage somehow made my position in the company more fragile; that for all my education at one of the best drama conservatoires in the country, and successfully auditioning for the RSC's casting directors, I was being done a favour. It was my frangible sense of position in the company that would lead me to stay silent when a casting controversy emerged.

It was during a meet-and-greet when I first heard the newly appointed Artistic Director of the RSC, Gregory Doran, refer to the play he was directing that season in the company's smaller theatre, *The Orphan of Zhao*, as the 'Chinese Hamlet'. The phrase would be repeated in press marketing and reviews. It marked the first time that the RSC had performed a Chinese play. Hot on the tail of an all-South Asian production of *Much Ado About Nothing*, hopes were raised in the British theatre community that this would represent an opportunity for British South-East Asians, who are sorely under-represented both on and off stage in the industry, to perform major roles at the prestigious company. Those hopes were soon dashed, however, when the casting was announced. Of a cast of seventeen, only three were South-East Asian and all were playing minor roles. The Arts Council England grant to the company in 2010–2011 was £15.6m, representing 48 per cent of the company's total income. Actors and other creatives from the South-East Asian diaspora began to voice their disappointment that, in this landmark production, they were being so poorly represented. The Arts Council is funded by taxpayers and many felt disappointed in the RSC's oversight in failing to recognise the importance of inclusive casting decisions for the show. As the criticisms grew from within the company, however, Doran dismissed the scrutiny, bemoaning how unfair planned protests were for those who had already been cast in the show. He would later anger his critics by countering that the RSC had auditioned 'lots and lots' of South-East Asian actors for the show, and in some cases made offers that were turned down, countering, 'I have to say, partly, it feels a bit like sour grapes.' The RSC would go on to blame the restriction of cross-casting, where actors perform in multiple roles across shows during a season, as one of the main factors for a lack of diversity, begging the question, 'Why must these actors only be cast in the Chinese play?'

I was uncomfortable with the choices that had been made, but I felt I was in no position to critique an institution that, it had been made clear to me, I should feel grateful just to be a part of. And so my criticisms went unvoiced.

Having later worked with Doran and the RSC years later in a tour of China and New York, I can attest to his being a talented director and a kind man on a personal level. Unfortunately, the insidiousness of racism on an institutional level means that oversight and insensitive decisions can belie your personal character. I discussed the controversy with Paapa who, in 2016, went on to play the titular role in *Hamlet* for the RSC to critical acclaim.

'It's just wild. It's absolutely wild. To even think about how that went down. It was a different time. Even though it was only eight years ago. But it's really gross to look back on now. It's embarrassing to be on the wrong side of history.'

When I asked him whether he felt able to voice his concerns about the company when we were newly graduated or if it would have jeopardised his career, he was his usual candid self.

'One hundred per cent. I wouldn't have played Hamlet. But then it's about power. I would feel comfortable doing it *now* because I don't *need* to be at the RSC. You can say you'll deny me a job in the future, but I can look at myself in the mirror. Can you?'

The complicated relationship I have with the company is comparable to that of the one I have with my country. The doors and possibilities that have been available to me because of the top-quality talents I have watched, worked alongside and had the opportunity to grow from are countless and I will forever feel a deep affinity to the company. But it is this same affinity that makes me so aware of its potential to do more, to be more inclusive, to pass the ladder back down and open the doors to countless others. As a national institution, known the world over, it should be accessible to all British people. Nevertheless I share Essiedu's sense of professional risk in speaking up for what you believe to be the right thing, and also the degree of protection that our later successes have gifted us both. But for many actors that sense of protection can feel very transient.

During the Black Lives Matter protest of 2020, John Boyega would attend the march and voice his support for the global fight against racism. Having starred as a principal actor in several *Star Wars* films and carried several others as the protagonist, I felt a deep sense of empathy with the words he chose to tearfully close his speech.

'I'm speaking to you from my heart. Look, I don't know if I'm going to have a career after this, but fuck that.'

Britain is changing, as it always has been throughout its storied history. The responsibility to 'build a bridge', however, surely lies with us now, in this moment, not as some burden to be passed onto the nascent shoulders of British children at some deferred point in the future. As much as we must listen to those who are excluded and give them a platform to be heard, we must also acknowledge the privilege and protection that we have been afforded to allow us to effect change now. Our silence enables others to believe that their behaviour is acceptable and will be tolerated because it *is* tolerated. We have a long history of diminishing and silencing the voices of those who have not been heard. For our future to be different from our past, we must do what has never been done before. So what comes next?

8

A New Normal

'We fail to read the serial killer accurately because
he is an embodiment of society's dominant values.
As a culture we are so unable to admit or recognise
the connection between our dominant forms of
masculinity and violent misogynistic crimes that we
must attribute motive to them besides masculinity.'

Of Men and Monsters: Jeffrey Dahmer and the
Construction of the Serial Killer,
RICHARD TITHECOTT

During a press junket in February 2019, Liam Neeson gave an interview for his new film *Cold Pursuit* with *The Independent*. After being asked to give more insight into his character Nels Coxman's desire for revenge after his son is killed by a drug cartel, Neeson made a confession that would spark global controversy and outrage. In his work on the *Taken* series, the Hollywood star had already featured in three revenge-centric movies and had done similar press junkets for them all without ever mentioning the story that he was about to tell; perhaps that was why it was such a surprise to hear him recount an incident that was so shocking. He stated that about forty years ago, he had just come back from overseas when a close female friend told him that she had been raped. According to Neeson:

'She handled the situation of the rape in the most extraordinary way. But my immediate reaction was ... I asked did she know who it was? No. What colour were they? She said it was a Black person. I went up and down areas with a cosh, hoping I'd be approached by somebody – I'm ashamed to say that, and I did it for maybe a week, hoping some "Black bastard" would come out of a pub and have a go at me about something, you know? So that I could ... kill him. It took me a week, maybe a week and a half, to go through that. She would say, "Where are you going?" and I would say, "I'm just going out for a walk." You know? "What's wrong?" "No no, nothing's wrong."'

After his co-star Tom Bateman interjected in disbelief, 'Holy shit!', Neeson's response was, 'It's awful. But I did learn a lesson from it, when I eventually thought, "What the fuck are you doing", you know?'

He would go on to explain how his time growing up in Northern Ireland amidst the Troubles had given him an insight into the cycles of violence.

'I understand that need for revenge, but it just leads to more revenge, to more killing and more killing, and Northern Ireland's proof of that. All this stuff that's happening in the world, the violence, is proof of that, you know. But that primal need, I understand.'

Even in this profoundly disturbing confession of his 'primal need' for revenge, the interview that Neeson gave was deeply unsettling for a number of reasons. I was not convinced that even decades after the event, he had understood where his seemingly 'primal' urge for violence had come from. The actor, in trying to ascertain the identity of the perpetrator of the heinous act of violence against his friend, asked only two questions: whether they were acquainted and what colour the attacker was. For Neeson, that was all the information he needed to start wandering the streets with murderous intent for a week or more hoping a 'Black bastard' would start a confrontation with him.

The implication by Neeson is that all Black men are the same. All rapists. All responsible for the violence and trauma enacted on his friend – and therefore all justifiable potential victims of his retribution. The implication from Neeson is that not only are Black men sexual predators, but they are also innately violent, liable to set upon a stranger unprovoked so that Neeson might mete out his 'justice' against all Black men. Ironically, Neeson is not alone in his failure to scrutinise his actions or to recognise where his primal need to enact violence stems from, with many deeming it a personal failing. Even the reporter who broke the story of the actor's violent confession would seek to explain and justify his 'brief desire for such random, violent revenge' by contacting psychologists who attempted to explain Neeson's mindset. This would be the tone adopted by Neeson and others in the media who sought to explain away his actions. Michelle Rodriguez, who appeared in the film *Widows* with the actor, would attest that it was impossible to lay the charge of racism at Neeson's door because of his performance in the film, perhaps unaware of the violence that Black women have faced from white men in the United States' complicated history.

'It's all fuckin' bullshit. Liam Neeson is not a racist. Dude, have you watched *Widows*? His tongue was so far down Viola Davis's throat. You can't call him a racist ever. Racists don't make out with the race that they hate, especially in the way he does with his tongue – so deep down her throat. I don't care how good of an actor you are. It's all bullshit. Ignore it. He's not a racist.'

Rodriguez would not be alone in supporting the actor. Whoopi Goldberg said in his defence, 'People walk around sometimes with rage, that's what happens. Is he a bigot? No. I've been around a lot of real bigots. I can say this man is not one.'

In Britain, Neeson would find an unlikely ally in former footballer John Barnes, who declared that he 'deserved a medal' for making the unsettling confession. The extent to which Neeson did not realise the potential harm his words had caused, however, was evident when he appeared on

Good Morning America to further clarify his comments and attempt to exonerate himself. After Neeson's conscience had caught up with him and he recognised the repulsiveness of his actions, he sought outside help. 'I did seek help. I went to a priest who heard my confession – I was raised a Catholic. I had two very good friends that I talked to, and, believe it or not ... power walking. Two hours every day to get rid of this.'

Reading the interview and the subsequent media coverage was deeply chilling for me. In that one confession I felt the distillation of my mother and father's worst fears for me as a young Black man in Britain – fears that I was powerless to defend or insulate myself against. There is an intersection of the personal and the political that stalks Black people in Britain; an immutable shadow that is ever present, but one that can be less or more visible depending on the brightness of the light that is shone. Reading that interview, I was struck by the futility of my personal responsibility in the face of narratives that had been told about Black men for centuries in the interests of jingoistic patriotism.

As a young man who counts himself a practising Catholic in the twenty-first century, with all the challenges that come with that, I understand the appeal of a personal confession and absolution. But the notion that a 'primal need' for revenge against *any* Black man might serve to sate the appetite of wounded male pride is not merely a personal moral failing, as so many hoped to paint it: it is the end result of a society that views Black men as an existential threat to white women and, by proxy, white masculinity. Unfortunately, 'Our Fathers' and 'Hail Marys' at confession or racking up steps on a pedometer will not be the cure. Although I'm grateful that Neeson did not murder anyone, Barnes's assertion that such a confession warrants the giving of a medal is setting the bar for what we can and should expect from one another at a subterranean level.

There is no doubt that the confession does represent a recognition of personal failing; that much is apparent. What is equally apparent, though, is the rush to diminish the possibility that any remnants of those racist beliefs are still maintained, as journalists, fellow actors and broadcasters attempted to leap into the brave new world of a 'post-racial' twenty-first century by failing to acknowledge that Neeson's 'primal need' is not solely his own, but rather that he is the product of a broader society that is still grappling with race. The tempting solution to sacrifice Neeson as single-handedly responsible for his reprehensible attitudes removes the onus from us as a society to understand and interrogate where his racist, toxic masculine preconceptions originated.

As a white man, the awareness of that struggle can feel jarring and limiting; as a Black man, I have had it as long as I can remember. How then might we begin to move through and past our storied and complex history, and how can we ensure that we move in the right direction? Before anything else we need to make sure that we understand how far we have come on our journey and how we got there. After this, it is imperative to ensure that the compass you are relying on to navigate is not only properly calibrated, but that the cardinal directions are honestly denoted.

In her seminal book *Caste: The Origins of Our Discontents*, Isabel Wilkerson compares the necessity of understanding the history of the nation with the medical history that one supplies to a doctor, without which the doctor will not dare attempt to diagnose whatever ails us.

> Looking beneath the history of one's country is like learning that alcoholism or depression runs in one's family or that suicide has occurred more often than might be usual or, with the advances in medical genetics, discovering that one has inherited the markers of a BRCA mutation for breast cancer. You don't ball up in a corner with guilt or shame at these discoveries. You don't, if you are wise, forbid any mention of them. In fact, you do the opposite. You educate yourself. You talk to people who have been through it and to specialists who have researched it. You learn the consequences and obstacles, the options and treatment. You may pray over it and meditate over it. Then you take precautions to protect yourself and succeeding generations and work to ensure that these things, whatever they are, don't happen again.

There is a hope that if we stop talking about race or gender then the issues that accompany them in society will quietly fade into the background; that by ignoring disparities in health and educational outcomes or employment opportunities, they will inevitably dissipate. The impulse behind such sentiments is understandable. After all, racist cis-heteropatriarchal narratives have been around for centuries in not only Britain but across the world. In the face of the weight of such history, the mountain of change may seem insurmountable. Nevertheless, it must still be ventured. There is no alternative. Much like in Wilkerson's doctor's office, it would be negligent of us to deny our children the right to a fair start at life because the conversation with our medical physician was deemed 'too uncomfortable'.

In 2020, Opinium ran a poll in the aftermath of the Black Lives Matter protests in which more than half of UK respondents believed that the protests increased racial tensions in the country. This is not an unreasonable response. The ugly history of our nation has been hidden from us rather than observed, understood and learned from. The actor Will Smith summed up the matter in a pithy sentence: 'Racism is not getting worse; it's getting filmed.' Far too often, I have had it communicated to me through body language or pregnant silences, and other times more vocally, that my discussion of the issues of race and gender are somehow 'gauche' or that I'm 'playing the race card'. I acknowledge the tedium of having to discuss these issues, especially because it feels like a family history that we have all inherited. As boring as it might be to hear it discussed, it is even more boring to experience the consequences of. We may not all be affected in exactly the same way, but it is naïve to think that we are not all affected. It also feels like crude self-interest if we don't feel compelled to change a system merely because it doesn't affect our lives; or worse, that we benefit from it.

Jane Elliott, the notable anti-racist educator, poses a scenario, asking her audience, 'Of those of you who are white, if you would be happy to be treated in the same way Black members of our society are treated, raise your hand.' As her audience invariably keeps their hands static, Elliott proves her point. We are aware of the various injustices in our society, even if the systemic nature of such challenges are presented simultaneously as legacies of the past to which we bear no responsibility and as insurmountable challenges. The philosopher John Rawls suggested a framework for law making that came to be known as the 'veil of ignorance' or 'original position', where the only truly fair laws and socioeconomic agendas were those created behind a hypothetical veil, before the lawmakers had any subjective knowledge of what their position in society would be.

Rawls's rationale was that if we were to be unaware of the race, class, gender or many of the other determining factors to life outcomes one might be born into, then we would strive towards creating a society that was as inclusive and as just as possible, as we would be unable to rely on our personal, subjective privileges. In my own experience, it was my maternal grandfather's confrontation with the reality of a Nigerian son-in-law and mixed-race grandchildren that forced him to reconsider whether the stories he had been told – and in turn believed about people of African origin – were accurate. As Britain shifts and evolves, I find myself questioning how I might ensure that the young Black men who follow me, be they my brother, cousins, nephew or, God-willing, one day children of my own, are not restricted as I have found myself to be? How might we move towards a new normal?

In the summer of 2020, ahead of the airing of its third series, the BBC Three show *Famalam* tweeted a sketch from the upcoming episode that would go viral. The skit featured a satirical Jamaican version of the quiz programme *Countdown* and invoked stereotypes about Jamaican people. One such stereotype was the figure of a man in shadow behind the familiar *Countdown* clock face. 'When you hear the Countdown conundrum, its letters, numbers, hell of a cock, boom,' are the lyrics to the mock theme tune, which as it reaches its conclusion is accompanied by the inferred silhouette of an oversized penis on the clock face. The sketch would draw the ire of the Jamaican foreign minister who declared that she would be writing to the BBC to complain about the sketch, calling the show 'outrageous and offensive to the incredible country which I am proud to represent along with every Jamaican at home and within our diaspora'. Despite the international attention that the comedy skit drew, BBC Three controller Fiona Campbell defended the show.

'*Famalam*'s now in its third series and its very successful creators have had some BAFTA wins for them. It's not
malicious humour and I think if you followed [the show] on
social, the creators said they're poking fun at all stereotypes.
There isn't malice in the type of content.'

Many online pointed to a cast and creative team that
heavily featured Black talent, suggesting that this entitled
them to make these jokes. Yet watching the clip, I still felt
unsettled. Ultimately, the racist trope of Cis Black men
having oversized penises was still being invoked. This
narrative that has been used as a tool to dehumanise and
justify the subjugation of Black people globally was being
replicated on British television as the world reeled from the
global protests of people declaring in the streets that 'Black
Lives Matter'.

If we are to truly strive for equality and inclusivity for all
Britons, we must be more aware of the narratives that we
are perpetuating. As race is such a multifaceted, composite
construction, many of us might like to believe, much like
Campbell, that a lack of 'malicious humour' is enough to
not be damaging. Intention can be an important factor but,
after centuries of 'malunions' in our education and societal
narratives, the unconscious repercussions of our actions can
be just as harmful.

Imagine a race around an athletics track. Without the
knowledge of the difference in the radius of each lane, it
might look like each competitor should start at the same
point. However, the curvature of the lanes of the track is

such that the inside track is a quarter of a mile, or four hundred metres, while the radius of lane eight is just over four hundred and fifty metres. Taking this difference into account is why those on the inside track are seemingly staggered back when the racetrack is perceived overhead. If, however, the race were to continue and as two athletes raced hard alongside each other, Athlete A violently swung their arm and caught Athlete B in the mouth, one might be tempted to call it foul play. However, Athlete A might protest their innocence and claim it was unintentional, which it may well have been. However, lap after lap, Athlete A's erratic arm movements continually connect with Athlete B, causing physical pain, injury and impeding their progress. With each lap around the track, Athlete B might feel increasingly more frustrated by Athlete A's protestations of innocence and ignorance at having caused any pain. After all, this is how Athlete A had always been taught to run and they would never intentionally assault another competitor, not like some of the other athletes. In fact, the very accusation that they might causes deep offence to Athlete A, and they claim that Athlete B is always complaining about their treatment on the racetrack.

I have been each of those athletes; both causing harm and receiving it. The majority of the time I have caused harm, it has been unintentional and I have just been trying to power my arms and legs through life, unaware of the damage I have caused; and while I have certainly encountered those who would *purposefully* seek to injure me, I do believe that in most instances, most people are just trying to run their own race. I also believe that we can teach, listen and learn from each other about the damage and harm that we have intentionally and unintentionally received and caused in the past, and that it's only by boldly and bravely doing this that we can begin this journey to our new normal.

A few years back, as I sat in my cousin's living room to celebrate a birthday in the family, I would have a discussion that would prove instructive and informative. It was a warm summer's day, which meant this particular family gathering of around thirty adults and children could spill out into the garden where the children made full use of the outdoor space to adorn their 'Sunday bests' with grass stains. This created a rare child-free lacuna, during which I teased my cousin David, who had on this rare occasion done the bulk of the cooking. He had been press-ganged into the situation after dismissing his sister's efforts. She was usually the one who would spend countless hours preparing jollof rice and chicken and other traditional Nigerian dishes for the family to enjoy. His insistence that 'it's not such a big deal', when none of us could recall him ever contributing much in the kitchen department, had seen the rest of the family call him on his boastful claim, resulting in him sweating away into the early hours as he struggled to prepare the food in time for the party. As the women of the family found themselves taking a rare break, I asked David whether the immensity of this task had given him a newfound respect for the work his sister had usually undertaken.

It was at this point that an older uncle interjected that even though David should know how to provide for himself, it was not his job to cook for the family; that was the job of the women alone, and in fact his wife should have taken this burden from him. As he spoke, I could feel some of the younger cousins begin to bristle, caught between wanting to interject and filial piety. I empathised as I felt my own sensitivities inflame. Nevertheless, he continued on and, as he did, I found myself joining the conversation. I wasn't agreeing, merely encouraging him to keep speaking. In asking him to expand upon his position, I had given him permission to share his experiences and fears. The impromptu sermon he delivered from the sofa – one that could have been entitled, 'A man works for the home, a woman's home is her work' – began to reveal the deep insecurity he felt about the loss of cultural history and connection to back home.

'If a man is being paid less than a woman, does that mean that he should be doing the housework?' I asked.

'No. In fact, she should even come home and make sure that he feels like a man by looking after him properly. Otherwise, he will feel like he has failed.'

The bemused laughter that this drew across the gender divide from the rest of the family demonstrated the fragility of this position. But that did not make it any less felt or believed. Despite our contrasting views, the honest exchange and frank discussion was infused with listening and love. It was perhaps this love and sense of having been heard that allowed my uncle to be shifted when one of my aunties, who had been relatively taciturn up until this point interjected.

'I spend all day working at the call centre. Then I return home and I am expected to look after the children and their education. On top of that, I am expected to maintain the house with cooking and cleaning. Is our work not equally tiring? Why should we, as husband and wife, expect more or less from each other if we are partners?'

My uncle paused as we all patiently waited for an answer, sensing that we had arrived at the heart of the matter. The four-word response was telling: 'Because it is tradition.'

The Nigerian novelist my father relished introducing me to, Chinua Achebe, once said in an interview with *Paris Review*, 'Until the lions have their own historians, the history of the hunt will always glorify the hunter.' The cultural erasure that Nigeria, as well many other parts of the world affected by Western colonialism, has experienced has created a curious relationship with tradition and culture. Growing up, I was acutely aware of the tension from both the Irish and Nigerian sides of my family, of not wanting to lose our cultural identity. As my uncle spoke about what he perceived to be a woman's place in the home, and as we listened and allowed him space to expound, it became clear that his determination to maintain cultural norms in a country that had denigrated, marginalised and patronised the traditions he held close to his identity was rooted in fear.

Although our previous conversations had been infused with trepidation on both sides, as this one wound up, my uncle and his younger interlocutors left with an enhanced knowledge of each other. Previous experience had led him to think I was a sometimes impetuous youth with too quick a tongue and a sometimes careless lack of regard for my heritage, whereas my previous experience had led me to characterise him as somebody who held onto outdated beliefs that bordered on being bigoted and intolerant. While both opinions might have had a degree of truth to them, human beings are defined by the pluralities of their experiences, often shaped by their contradictions. Neither my uncle nor I are binary creatures, and it does us both a disservice to classify each other as such. It is in fact our deep, shared passion for our heritage that has greatly informed both of our lives and how we decide to live them.

The younger Obi would have been frustrated by my uncle's exordium and immediately entered defence mode in preparation for what I saw as an attack on the enlightened, liberal, moral norms that I considered an essential part of who I am as a person. My patience would have worn thin as we butted heads, determined to score a victory and, by superior logic and moral assuredness, cudgel my uncle, some decades my senior, into the idyllic paradise of my liberal viewpoint. The arrogance of youth! This time, due to the idiosyncratic circumstances of this particular gathering, I had the space to listen and not just hear my uncle. Days after our conversation, I found myself still thinking about those four words: *Because it is tradition*. The essayist Ralph Waldo Emerson once wrote, 'Knowledge is the antidote to fear.' I wondered if my uncle would still be so worried about the loss of tradition, so fearful about the place of the Nigerian man if, as Achebe wrote, we became our own historians.

My cousin David who had catered for us at that family gathering grew up and went to university in Nigeria before moving to London. A few years into living here, a newlywed friend of his came to visit from Lagos with his wife. While having dinner, David asked his friend's wife about the current state of politics in Lagos, which his friend promptly shut down. '*Nawao*, David, why do we need to hear my wife's opinion? She's speaks too much already.' When David tried to insist on listening to her, his friend chastised him. 'You see? You've been hanging with these English people too much, oh! You are now woman wrapper, *kai!*'

David was shocked. A 'wrapper' is the word used to describe a colourful piece of cloth that both men and more often women wrap around themselves in both formal and informal attire. A 'woman wrapper' however, David tells me, is the expression used about a man who allows himself to seemingly be controlled or dominated by a woman. David was bewildered to hear these words coming from his friend, and even more so to have the idea of listening to the words of a friend at the dinner table dismissed as an English affectation merely because she was a woman.

'I really thought that it was something that was fading, you know? Maybe our parents' generation. But it shocked me to hear my age-mate saying this.'

Once more I was struck by the idea of history and storytelling: who are the storytellers and who is the audience? The effects of the British and other colonial forces are still felt to this day beyond the more obvious and publicised narratives of destabilised governments, pillaging of natural resources by Western interests and loans with crippling interest rates that have kept Africa dependent on Western countries to this day. Both David's old classmate and my uncle believed that they must hold tight to a past narrative and feared that to somehow move forward or be progressive was an abandonment of 'traditional' Nigerian values. How ironic that the very act of positioning themselves as apparently anti-colonialist still accepted the narrative that Nigerian values must be diametrically opposed to British when many of the laws and norms with regard to sexuality and gender had been imposed by a Victorian-era colonial ideology.

Just like my uncle, I love my heritage. Yet I found myself struggling to reconcile how I could embrace it fully and wholeheartedly when it seemed so counter to my instincts about unlearning internalised racism and sexism. Thinking about the younger members of my family, not least my niece and nephew, I had often worried that there would be a contention between patriarchal, hetero, cisgendered-roles and expectations that were a part of our family's culture and the more equitable upbringing my brother was insistent on giving them. But as we sat in that too stuffy living room, listening to and hearing each other for the first time in a long time, I found myself optimistic that the idea of what it meant to be a Black man *could* shift and need not be a fixed notion.

The Greek philosopher Aristotle wrote, 'Excellence, then, being of these two kinds, intellectual and moral, intellectual excellence owes its birth and growth mainly to instruction, and so requires time and experience, while moral excellence is the result of habit or custom.'

Humanity is always evolving, growing and changing as, I believe, it seeks to better itself. That is not unique to British history; it is a maxim that holds true globally, cross culturally. It is a testament to human complexity and nuance that we can hold what seem to be polar-opposite understandings at the same time and not be crippled with intellectual inertia. Often, I'll hear friends wistfully daydream that 'they wish they had lived in Victorian times'. Yet, there is no time in human history that I would rather live in than the present. Despite the seemingly turbulent politics of recent years, the advances made in living outcomes, life expectancy and the sheer wealth of information at our disposal all suggest that the world is moving in a more hopeful direction. Many hold the contradiction of knowing that the present day with all of its benefits is a hard-fought departure from a past that was less just and fair, while also believing that our work is now done. Surely we don't believe that our present day is perfect and without need or space for improvement?

The 'time and experience' and 'habit or custom' that Aristotle writes about is a clarion call to us all to maintain our excellence and recognise that while we still have a past that informs us, we cannot rest on our laurels. It wasn't until 1975 that women were allowed to open a bank account in their own name, and it would take until 1995 until the first far-reaching act that legislated on discrimination towards disabled people would be passed – and it would be 2014 before the first same-sex marriage took place in Britain. The 'Greatness' of Britain is as much about the promise and potential of our future as it is about our past. Creating a world that is fairer for everyone is at the heart of that. But where to even begin?

A person may be apolitical, but politics is never impersonal. The very word 'political' has its origins in the writing of Aristotle, whose *Politiká* literally means 'the things concerning the polis [city]'. Society has, fortunately, progressed and our understanding of democracy has evolved over the centuries. As much as we might choose to excuse ourselves from the responsibilities of 'politics' as an idea, it permeates everything. It is the history we are taught in our schools. It is the healthcare, justice and welfare structures that we will all avail ourselves of. It is the films we watch and the media we consume. There is a saying that 'decisions are made by those who show up'. For a large part of Britain's history, those who 'showed up' were by design a select few. If there is no disadvantage to those who are in power ignoring your opinion, then they will continue to do so.

Only in the rarest instances of human history has power been given away freely. The term 'status quo' is a shortening of the Latin phrase *'status quo ante bellum'*; literally translated as 'the situation as it existed before the war'. While not every divestment of power requires a physical war per se, there is a necessary struggle that causes those who have previously thought one way to shift their thinking and compromise. For those who have always had power, maintaining the status quo or ensuring that they benefit from it has always been easier, because they have always had access to other people in power, making their ability to have their personal – or should we say political – interests served. Those who have not always been heard or have been marginalised and pushed to the side have had to get creative to ensure that people pay attention. They have had to disrupt the usual power structures to effect change. For something to happen which has never happened before, often something must be done which has never been done before. In the summer of 2020, that was precisely what happened.

After footage emerged of George Floyd being slowly killed by a police officer kneeling on his neck for more than eight minutes during an arrest, there were protests in more than sixty countries and two thousand cities in support of Black Lives Matter. Across industries, the murder sparked a global reckoning with the anti-Black racism that was still being perpetuated across the world. Although it was initially centred on police brutality and a demand for criminal justice reform, focusing on community funding rather than an increasingly militarised police, for the first time in my lifetime the idea that Black people suffered racism in many different aspects of their lives did not seem like a fringe idea.

As I marched through central London, I was heartened by what I witnessed. The march was not solely made up of people from the Black community, nor was it just the exuberant youth who felt fired up and compelled to protest. Rather, I saw a coalition of sorts that crossed age, race and gender. For the first time in Britain, I felt quietly hopeful that this flashpoint might be the spark, the catalyst for change for which it suddenly seemed there was an appetite. One by one, I received texts from friends who were checking in on my mental health and wondering how I was coping having witnessed this brutal murder. My social media pages were rife with people proudly boasting about acquiring their new anti-racist book and how essential it was. Companies began posting black squares on their social media accounts with #BlackLivesMatter as the caption. All of a sudden, it seemed there was cause for optimism, a possibility that change was imminent, a watermark moment from which there was no going back. But past experience can make cynics of the best of us.

I was grateful for the education that my friends,

colleagues and acquaintances were engaging in. I was thankful for the renewal of my optimism. But my feelings were divided. Receiving the clumsy attempts at comfort, I found myself resentful. I was resentful at the slow arrival to this point of demanding change. I was vexed that it was *this* murder of an unarmed Black man that had caused a global outrage. Among the countless messages I received, I detected a subtext of 'at least we're over here' – an idea that British racism is somehow better, less deleterious. What I heard was, 'You can be grateful that you're here and not being shot by the police.' How tragically low a bar for us to congratulate ourselves on meeting.

For those who experience racism in this country, we are still in the midst of the war, struggling to get through the other side of the status quo. It's painful to feel that those you live and work alongside, care for and love, do not perceive or acknowledge the pain that you experience. It is a luxury to learn about rather than experience the effects of racism: the fear, the consistent neurosis, the consistent microaggressions that are reminders of your seemingly outsider status. As a 6 ft 2, 115 kg Black man in this country, I felt like I understood the need for change. Yet it was precisely my understanding of how I was perceived that would soften my outlook.

My brothers all learned to ride a bike when they were about six years old. Setting off as a trio, they would cycle to the local park and I would trail behind on foot, struggling to keep up. My father, who had taught my brothers to ride, had work trips abroad that would render him unavailable for my two-wheeled education after school. So, my Irish grandmother spoiled me, as she always did, buying me a bright-blue bike with stabilisers for Christmas in 1994. Time went on and I found my passions in performing and rugby robbing me of most of my free time, while my brothers' bikes fell into disrepair. The ceremonial hand-me-down was skipped, as I lacked the requisite skill to make use of either. The years went by, and as I approached my teens, I would politely refuse offers to ride friends' bikes because I didn't want to embarrass myself. I would learn one day but today, today wasn't the day.

On the occasions that friends would bring their bikes to the park and insist I had a ride, I would bluff, pushing myself off the floor and gliding a few metres, perhaps down a hill. But when it came to pedalling, or being able to steer, I was terrified and thought I would get it all wrong. It would take until the summer of my GCSEs for me to corner my eldest brother Chi and ask him to teach me to ride. At first my request was laughed off, as my brother looked on incredulously at my inability to hold my balance. But, sensing my vulnerability, he accompanied me to our nearest green space in north London, Whittington Park. It was there, aged sixteen – while my friends celebrated their freedom from exams with underage drinking in the park – that my older brother soothed the shame I felt in my lack of coordination with his kindness. Not that I was a particularly good student. Where most children are young enough to bounce back from the damage both to body and ego, each fall would set me back from my progress as I imagined everybody looking at me and staring at my six-foot frame on a second-hand bike.

In reality, nobody was the slightest bit interested apart from my brother, who had seemingly inherited the vast reserves of patience that my dad so often demonstrated. As he ran alongside me, I found myself pedalling and occasionally gaining my balance for periods at a time. His two-word mantra as I attempted to find my spot in the middle was 'Be brave', repeated with a consistency that bordered on the tedious. If, in my moment of unsteadiness and vulnerability, my brother had laughed in my face, I would have resisted riding my bike. I might have made excuses about my ability to ride, terrified of the further embarrassment of hurting myself and my pride. There can be a temptation to, much like Chi initially did, believe that everybody can ride a bike, forgetting that there was once a time when we had to learn and it was awkward and painful and tedious.

When those messages from my friends and acquaintances, colleagues and past lovers came flooding in, in what seemed like an indulgent deluge of their new-found awareness that Black lives really do matter, I believe it was understandable for me to feel frustrated, vexed and incredulous. The narratives that we have been taught about race and gender are both broad and specific, wide reaching yet deep rooted. The internalised sexism, racism and homophobia that many of us grapple with are products of the society that we live in. Knowing this fact does not mean that our society is unloving or incapable of change. I may believe myself to be free from certain problematic ideas about what it is to be a Black man, but all of that is because, at some point in time, somebody had the grace and patience to ensure I might not repeat the same transgressions.

There was once a time when I did not know better. Accepting that is the first step to acknowledging that we are capable of change because we can all admit that we are not perfect. Winston Churchill once said, 'To improve is to change, so to be perfect is to have changed often.' Our potential then for change is the source of our excellence. Without the kindness, patience, understanding and forgiveness of those whom I may have consciously or unconsciously harmed, I would not be where I am today. All I can hope for is the capacity to treat others with the same level of compassion and capacity for growth that I would wish to be treated with. But this does not excuse my actions or the intrinsic violence of words that have been steeped in misogyny or racism. Ultimately, I cannot expect the burden of those who have been victimised to assume the role of the educator, relying on the seemingly superhuman, saint-like forbearance of marginalised communities. And just as I cannot on a personal level expect this level of stoicism, if we seek to change the status quo it is incumbent upon us as a society to address our history, our present and how we would like to go into the future. We have a choice to join that awkward, unsettling struggle to create a fairer world and a new normal for ourselves and each other, no matter how belatedly. We can either choose to resist that appetite for a more equitable society out of a sense of misplaced pride, or we can accept that we will occasionally fall short, slip up and yet keep driving towards a brighter future all driven by those two words: 'Be brave.'

As thousands took to the streets in cities across the country in support of Black Lives Matter, their awakening to some of the systemic issues that permeate our society created a new-found sense of the power of everyday citizens to change policy in both public and private spheres. The point of a protest is to disrupt and cause discomfort to our usual way of thinking. In this the BLM protests succeeded, shifting the conversation in an unprecedented fashion as conversations about everything from boardroom representation to the contents of the national curriculum came under scrutiny. As race came to the fore, organisations attempted to show their support for equal rights for all. For footballers in England, many showed their support by taking the knee. The gesture would be adopted across the country. Even as the BBC showed only highlights of football matches on *Match of the Day*, the sight of some of the highest-paid sports people in the country showing solidarity with this global movement was included in the edit, month after month.

However, watching these gestures, I couldn't help but feel like the momentum had stagnated. After what had been an unparalleled expression of unity, a spark of outrage had seemingly been reduced to a gesture. I was not alone in this diagnosis. Les Ferdinand, cousin of Rio and Anton, and director of football at QPR, defended his team discontinuing taking the knee, remarking, 'The message has been lost. It is now not dissimilar to a fancy hashtag or a nice pin badge ... Taking the knee will not bring about change in the game – actions will.'

For all of the pressure created by the protests and the public support for the cause of racial equality, I shared Ferdinand's concern that the 'taking of the knee', much like the posting of a black square on a social media channel, had the potential to become a token gesture, granting organisations the ability to dodge true accountability by doing the bare minimum. We had now all acknowledged the larger systemic issue; what was called for was specific action.

9

Making the Change

*For, on the one hand, it seemed to him that all men
work more zealously against their enemies than
they cooperate with their friends.*

Roman History, CASSIUS DIO

Tom Chigbo is a community organiser with Citizens UK.
He was also Cambridge University's first Black Student
Union President. He was in the post when the biggest student demonstration in a generation, 50,000 people in central
London, protested against the rise of student fees. He also
saw it result in failure. Analysing the failure of such a large
gathering, he began to look for ways to more productively
effect change, which was when he would find community
organising and Citizens UK. I told him about my frustration
with a perceived lack of concrete action from companies

who had shown little support for racial justice beyond a general raising of awareness. He was optimistic, but shared my reservations.

'A lot of these big moments are important and they can result in individual people becoming more educated, but that doesn't translate to comprehensive change for enough people. The problems that we are all facing are just too large. That frustration and education is important, but it's not everything. Players taking the knee, for instance, is a very good example of half of the journey. There is a public expression of the depth of feeling and support. But what is the FA specifically doing? Are there enough of us interested in both anti-racism and football who are doing enough to hold them to account to tangible change?'

I found myself beginning to doubt my individual ability to effect change if this was happening on such a public stage and making little impact. If not even celebrities and the highest-paid sports stars in the country can do anything, then surely those who have less of a platform have even less power and influence? More to the point, should celebrities be telling us what to do?

'First of all, I don't agree with this notion that because you're a sports star or an entertainer that you shouldn't have a voice. I think first and foremost you are a citizen. You should be just as engaged as any other citizen. Celebrities can and should participate as leaders. But there can be a complacency, where we treat celebrities almost as heroes who by dint of their being famous indicate widespread support and everyone else is just passive. All we are expected to do is minor acts like signing a petition. As long as we get the media coverage, because celebrities are talking about this thing it's a success. I think that's like a really inadequate form of change making. I don't actually think it's the best use of their platform, and is also slightly patronising to the rest of the general public. You have to start with the public. And start simple. One simple binary request. You "ask". Like Rashford.'

In June of 2020, at the height of the Covid-19 pandemic, Manchester United forward Marcus Rashford would put his football superstardom and clout behind a simple request. The footballer, who himself received free school meals as a schoolboy, began tweeting about the UK's poorest families who, struggling to pay utility bills, would struggle to put food on the table throughout the summer holidays. His 'ask' to Prime Minister Boris Johnson was easy to grasp. 1.3 million children were entitled to free school meals, which they would not receive during the holidays. Would the government change its mind about not offering vouchers for free meals during the summer holidays?

Although many attempted to rebuff him, including government ministers, the simplicity of the ask and the obvious moral clarity of the situation forced Boris Johnson's government into an embarrassing U-turn after more than 100,000 people signed a petition in support of Rashford's request. The simplicity of the demand was key. There was no room to manoeuvre or play politics. According to Chigbo, it had a galvanising effect on the public. 'He made it about specifics. Time and money – are you going to feed them, yes or no? That really helped. It had an invigorating effect on the public because the public then all focused on the specific issue and there was buy-in. Once they knew they could make a difference, they were then emboldened.'

As I looked at my own life and upbringing, I began to think what might have made it more equitable. Aware that not everybody can have a public platform the size of Rashford's, how could I begin to dismantle the toxic norms about Black masculinity that so permeated seemingly all parts of society? Was it even possible? Tom brought me back to reality with a bump.

'You can't get tangible change if you stay in the realm of the big complex problem. Those of us who want to change things need to hold the complexity of that larger problem, but focus on very specific tangible, oftentimes local things. If you can reduce it to a bite-sized issue, there can't be a review or study on it; it becomes a yes or no situation. If we can get into the habit of cutting the larger problem into manageably sized issues, that will go a long way to bringing about the necessary change.'

I realised he was right. I had seen several ambitious campaigns rise and then fall by the wayside as support petered out and goodwill evaporated. Why then did the summer protests of 2020 feel so different? What inspired such hope? I recalled the sense of unity on those marches and the bridging between demographics that normally would not coalesce to protest a singular cause. Tom elaborated on what I had instinctively picked up on. 'Often, the broader the coalition can be, the more seriously you are to be taken. Groups of people can be pigeonholed and dismissed. Decision makers begin to factor in pressure from certain groups as acceptable losses – *"they* moan about *that* thing" – whereas if you present a broad coalition and it's surprising, it's harder to dismiss. Some people believe only the people who think the same as me are my allies, to the exclusion of everyone else. But actually that limits your power. What is the broadest group of people that can support your one laser-focused goal? Once we tick off all the things on which we agree and work on that, then we can deal with the things that divide us. But we will have a deeper understanding of each other.'

Conversing with Tom, I was struck by the times in which the broadness of coalitions during the struggles for civil rights suddenly gave them credence. Perhaps the most notable example is President Lyndon B. Johnson's invocation of the phrase 'we shall overcome' when addressing both houses of Congress in 1965 in a nationally televised broadcast. Originally a gospel song, 'We Shall Overcome' became a central protest song to the US Civil Rights Movement. The President's open support of Dr Martin Luther King and the Selma-to-Montgomery marches to demonstrate African-Americans' constitutional right to vote – to the extent that he mobilised the Alabama National Guard to protect the protestors on the third day of marching – proved a signal of intent and a turning point in the

265

Civil Rights Movement. Yet that was an ocean away in a time that is often depicted in black and white. Are we to wait for a Dr King to emerge to lead the change that we need? Tom seemed to disagree.

'First and foremost, we have to accept that for you to have a good life as an individual, but then in a wider sense, for your family to have a good neighbourhood, or good local schools, or for you to ensure good work conditions, you have to join in. The second thing is that your personal circumstances will generally make you weak in your personal journey. But it's also where you derive your biggest strength. So start where you are. Do what you can in the community, organisation or institution that you are actively a part of. Any space that you are a part of where people come together can be a helpful tool in being a better citizen and improving the world in some way. When you are in that space, do what you can to bring people together to talk about what needs to change. For some people that could be in a formalised way of contacting your trade union at your employers. Some people don't have trade unions and it's just as basic as talking to somebody else. Perhaps it's the colleague that you share lunch with. Or it could be talking to other parents at the school gates and recognising that if the school sent the newsletter in a second language it would make life easier. If you a form a group who can go and have a conversation with the head teacher – that is the start.'

*

Kintsugi ('golden joinery'), also known as *kintsukuroi* ('golden repair'), is a Japanese art form of repairing broken pottery by mending areas that have broken with lacquer which has been mixed with precious metals such as gold, silver or platinum. There is an acceptance and an embracing in these art forms of the flaws and imperfections of an object that renders it more beautiful by virtue of those flaws.

In response to the reappraisal of British history in recent years, there has been a growing attempt to paint such evaluations as somehow talking the country down or being unpatriotic. I can't help but wonder how much more trust and respect we might have for each other, our politicians and our institutions if we collectively understood that we are imperfect humans, that our history is imperfect and that we have made such strides in our storied journey and will continue to do so. Our history cannot be, nor should it be, covered up. With the resilient nature of human history in mind, can we be brave enough to embrace our failures and allow them to be an instructive guide to a more united, accepting society?

The lawyer and activist Bryan Stevenson wrote: 'We are all broken by something. We have all hurt someone and have been hurt. We all share the condition of brokenness even if our brokenness is not equivalent ... Our shared vulnerability and imperfection nurtures and sustains our capacity for compassion. We have a choice. We can embrace our humanness, which means embracing our broken natures and the compassion that remains our best hope for healing. Or we can deny our brokenness, forswear compassion, and, as a result, deny our own humanity.'

The seventeenth-century poet John Donne once wrote:

> *No man is an island entire of itself,*
> *Every man is a piece of the continent,*
> *A part of the main*

Some four hundred years later, I find myself returning to this poem as a comfort, a sort of balm. There are those who would tell us that the state of the world is inexorable, immutable and fixed. They point to rising tensions in demographics and forecast a global schism in the fight for civil liberties. I cannot pretend that I haven't experienced everything from mean-spiritedness to outright violence – sometimes on account of the colour of my skin. But my lived experience, the fact that I am alive today, is a testament to the very human qualities of kindness, patience and the capacity to change. It is that experience that gives me cause to be hopeful because it *has* to get better. That experience is the voice that asserts, 'Be brave' when the odds seem insurmountable. We cannot afford to allow our sons and daughters and the generations who come after us to carry the burden of our inaction.

James Baldwin once wrote, 'Not everything that is faced can be changed, but nothing can be changed until it is faced.'

We can't know all the answers.

We will make mistakes.

We will do better.

Acknowledgements

Firstly, I must acknowledge that I have written a book, which is entirely mad. By its very nature, it is the culmination of the thoughts, ideas and musings of the people who have made me who I am today. These acknowledgements, then, cannot be exhaustive; but I carry you all in my heart.

Firstly, my God. Through him I can do all things. You are the substance of things hoped, the evidence of things not seen.

Mum and Dad, my admiration for your capacity for love, compassion and patience is never ending. You will always try to do whatever you can for whoever needs your help or care. I would not be half the man I am today without your kindness. My deepest wish is to make you proud and honour your dreams for us.

Alaeze, we are thick as thieves whenever we are together. You taught me to never back down and never to give up. You taught me to fight. Now I will never stop.

Chi, you have been a role model and a friend. A comfort in the darkest hours and a cheerleader on the biggest of stages. Rach, you're the best sister-in-law a man could ask for. RISK!

Grandpas Michael and John Joe, and Grandmas Lucy and Teresa, thank you for giving me roots to grow from and to hold strong in myself.

Sophie Austin, the dopest acting agent in the game. You were the oasis of calm in a world that became a tempest.

Hellie Ogden! One phone call literally changed everything. You have made literal dreams come true. You pushed, fine-tuned and championed me. Thank you Joe for the wedding invite.

Chris White, we just get each other. From countless meetings on zooms to nervous texts about elections, I have always felt safe, supported and seen.

Nathan and Dylan, my oldest friends and my group of awesomeness. We've come a long way from purple cassocks. Our far too infrequent lunches and talks make me a better man.

Nic, you were my rock as I wrote this. Your encouragement and patience made it all feel possible. I love you.

Our Triumvirate. Daniel, the cabeza-munching, Super-Smash-Bros-marathon-buddying foodie. Francis, the genius surgeon with sugar for kryptonite. Who else would I go under-aged clubbing with? DAGGER!

Cam, you are the biggest hearted man I know. Thank you for always reaching out. Love you always, my brother.

The Circle! What can I say? 'It Happens'. I have grown as a man because of our brotherhood (and that bloody WhatsApp group). Thank you for tolerating my constant posts and debates with our resident DA and my absence from parties because of this blasted career choice. May every man have a group like you to challenge them, comfort them and give them room and love to grow.

Katy Clark with an E, thank you for being a port in a storm, always far too empathetic and teaching me the meaning of kindness and forgiveness.

Madeline Sayet, those days with you as my roommate, blasting Disney tunes in the morning before going to Joe's and planning our global theatre takeover are some of the happiest of my life. You are always welcome home.

Jared, Louie, Omari! The Fantastic 4! Yo! We here! Long way from Glassworks, Chapel Market McDonald's and 'Festival of Plays'. Forward Movements Always! Jordanna, Natalie and Anna, thank you for always making the time and for dealing with our unique brand of crazy.

Ella, thank you for always challenging my perspectives. I've never been more thankful for a theatre trip than the Royal Court in 2015.

My godparents, Grainne and Nwabu, you have always supported me, whether sneakily flying over from Ireland or driving up to Scotland. Thank you for daring me to dream.

Cecily, you have one of the sharpest minds I know. Our wined chats refined so many of my ideas and thoughts.

Anthony, thank you for your bravery and your sharing and your undimmable light. You are radiance and joy. I am grateful to know you.

Zi, for our side DMs and surreptitious drinking at family functions. Deacon, you are always the hardest worker in the room. Your work ethic pushes me to keep going a little further for a little longer.

My Ham Fam! We did something special and those fifteen months gave me the courage to say what I needed to say. Thank you.

Mireille, our riverside walks were lifesavers.

Daniellé Scott-Haughton. One day on that darned bird app, I slid into your DMs asking to be your friend. I'm so glad you said yes. I couldn't have anticipated the love and fellowship I would receive from you. 'REACH OUT AND TOUCH!'

Bolu! You are awesome. Literally. You inspire awe. So effortlessly funny and incisive you are non-stop and yet you would take moments to check-in, reassure and calm.

Candice, you gave me permission. To dare to write. To freak out. To demand space.

Charlie, from 'Yoga with Adriene' to 5ks, we've made it. Thank you for always holding me to account and being the best drinking bud.

Thank you Dr. Nunn(s) for your help with medical terminology.

Mark, your ability to hold the grey areas and force me to sharpen my arguments is as infuriating as it is addictive. May we always have more time to put the world to rights.

Sharon Rose, you spoke to me when I was just starting, inviting me to 'believe in yourself'.

Tom Chigbo, your passion for organising and making a change gives me hope for the future. Thank you for talking with me.

Afua, you are an inspiration, a friend, a force. Thank you.

Simon Ashenden, James Trapmore and Evelyn Duah, you taught me to own my voice and stand in my power.

The folx at Bread by Bike (aka the best bakery in London), your sourdough sustained me.

To anybody and everybody who has ever supported, encouraged or shaped me. I am deeply grateful and eternally optimistic. You made this fool dare to dream he might be able to change somebody's mind or make a difference. May we all be so lucky to dream that.

Lastly, Onyedikachi. It is all for you. You are the brightest of lights. Never let this world tell you that the world is an oyster. Your world is every one of this blue planet's seven seas and so much more. I pray you always feel a sense of belonging to it all and most importantly, help others to find theirs.

Notes and Sources

2. THE MALUNION OF A FRACTURE

'In a malunion, a bone heals but not in the right position',

'Malunion and Nonunion', UPMC Orthopaedic
Care, www.upmc.com/services/orthopaedics

'Books are sometimes windows, offering views
of worlds',

Rudine Sims Bishop, *Mirrors, Windows and Sliding
Glass, Perspectives*: 'Choosing and Using Books for
the Classroom', Volume 6, Issue 3, Pages: 9–11, 1990

'I love sex, I love it. I can't do shit no more',

Bernie Mac, *Def Comedy Jam*, Season 2, Episode 1, 1992

'Forty-five per cent of men responded that they would like a larger penis',

> Bruce M. King, *Average-Size Erect Penis: Fiction, Fact, and the Need for Counseling*, 'Journal of Sex & Marital Therapy', Volume 47, Issue 1, 2021

3. SHACKLES

'In the end, we will remember not the words of our enemies, but the silence of our friends',

> from Martin Luther King's Steeler Lecture, 'The Trumpet of Conscience', November 1967 (also used as the title of a 1968 collection of lectures).

'You guys know about vampires?',

> 'Pulitzer prize-winning author Junot Díaz tells students his story', Brian Donohue, NJ Advance Media for www.nj.com, 21 October 2009

'only 15–20 per cent of US soldiers would fire at the enemy',

> Dave Grossman, *On Killing: The Psychological Cost of Learning to Kill in War and Society*, Black Bay Books, 1995

'Men are culturally programmed to take on the
warrior role',

> Tom Digby, *Love and War: How Militarism Shapes
> Sexuality and Romance*, Columbia University Press, 2014

'The majority of Negroes at present are discharged
soldiers',

> D. T. Aleifasakure Toummanah quoted in Jacqueline
> Nassy Brown, *Dropping Anchor, Setting Sail: Geographies of
> Race in Black Liverpool*, Princeton University Press, 2005

'The people here [in Liverpool] understand the negroes',

> unnamed police officer in 1919 quoted in
> Peter Fryer, *Staying Power: The History of
> Black People in Britain*, Pluto Press, 1984

'It is an instinctive certainty that sexual relations
between white women and coloured men',

> Sir Ralph Williams' letter to *The Times*, 1919, quoted
> in Peter J. Aspinall & Chamion Caballero, *Mixed Race
> Britain in the Twentieth Century*, Palgrave Macmillan, 2018

'almost invariably regret their alliance with a
coloured man',

Muriel E. Fletcher, *Report on an Investigation into the
Colour Problem in Liverpool and other Parts*, 1930

4. BLACK EXCEPTIONALISM AND BOUNTIES

'We must accept finite disappointment, but never lose
infinite hope',

Martin Luther King Jr., *In My Own Words*, a collection of
King's sermons, speeches and writings selected by his
widow Coretta Scott King, Hodder & Stoughton, 2002

'A Black man had never slapped a white man in an
American film',

'How we made In the Heat of the Night',
interview with Norman Jewison by Phil
Hoad, *The Guardian*, 22 November, 2016

'One ever feels his two-ness . . . '

W.E.B. DuBois, *The Souls of Black Folk:
Essays and Sketches*, Chicago, 1903

'£61,000 a year that government spends incarcerating each young male offender',

'Costs per place and costs per prisoner by individual prison', National Offender Management Service Annual Report and Accounts 2015–16, Ministry of Justice Information Release, www.gov.uk. 27 October 2016

'Taking away youth workers and safe spaces in the community',

'"Poverty of hope" has led to soaring knife crime says CEO of Britain's leading children's charity', *Evening Standard*, 8 March 2019

'Human rights experts from the UN would excoriate the report',

'UN Experts Condemn UK Commission on Race and Ethnic Disparities Report', United Nations Human Rights Office of the High Commissioner, www.ohchr.org, 19 April 2021

'Hell, we deliberately made the situation perfect',

Roger Ebert, 'Interview with Stanley Kramer', 1968, www.rogerebert.com

5. YOUNG, GIFTED AND BLACK

'Clyde Best, one of the few Black players blazing a trail',

> Clyde Best, *The Acid Test: A Life in Football – The Autobiography of Clyde Best*, De Coubertin Books, 25 August 2016

'legitimacy accrued to beating',

> Steven Pierce, *Punishment and the Political Body: Flogging and Colonialism in Northern Nigeria*. London: Routledge, 2001

'"Karate yes" or "Karate no"?',

> Robert Mark Kamen, *The Karate Kid*, released 1984

'Venus Williams is quizzed on her confidence',

> John McKenzie interview with Venus Williams, ABC *News Day One*, 1995 (YouTube)

'The truth is that racism has disappeared from the game',

> 'That Lukaku chant: it's open season on "football scum" again', Brendan O'Neill, www.spiked-online.com, 22 September 2017

'My brother Anton, the innocent party in all this',

'Terry is the biggest idiot ... he's never said sorry to Anton or me', Ben Jackson, *The Sun*, 13 September 2014

'I told him he had a choice: "You're my mate and you're John Terry's mate",

'Rio Ferdinand says he no longer speaks to Ashley Cole after he sided with John Terry in race row with his brother Anton', James Andrew, *MailOnline*, 14 September 2014

Danny Rose, 'I've had enough',

'Danny Rose on racism: Tottenham defender "can't wait to see the back of football"', www.bbc.co.uk/sport/football, 4 April 2019

'Regarding what was said at the Chelsea game',

'Raheem Sterling accuses media of "fuelling racism" after alleged abuse', Dominic Fifield, *The Guardian*, 9 December 2018

'For all the newspapers that don't understand',

'Manchester City's Raheem Sterling slams media coverage that "helps fuel racism"', www.espn.in

'As a coach, on reflection, I didn't really know how to deal with it',

Monday Night Football, Sky Sports, 'Full Sterling transcript: Neville, Carra discuss abuse', www.football365.com, 11 December 2018

'I am not going to stand up',

'Colin Kaepernick explains why he sat during national anthem', Steve Wyche, www.nfl.com/news, 27 August 2016

'Jesse Williams phrased it',

'Full transcript of Jesse Williams' powerful speech', www.time.com

'Conservative Chairman James Cleverly',

interview with Sophie Ridge, 'If the queen is happy, we should be happy', *Spectator*, 19 January 2020

'Nonviolence is a powerful and just weapon which cuts without wounding',

Martin Luther King Jr., Nobel Lecture, 11 December, 1964, www.nobelprize.org/prizes/peace/1964/king/lecture

'My thing was not really saving that man',

> 'BLM "band of brothers" hope rescue of counter-protestor sends message', Clea Skopeliti and Archie Bland, *The Guardian*, 15 June 2020

6. BLACK LOVE IS RADICAL

'*FHM*'s "100 Sexiest Women"',

> 'An Announcement Regarding FHM and Zoo Magazines', www.bauermedia.co.uk, 17 November 2015

'When it comes to Black females, who are the people who get their music played on pop radio?',

> 'Beyonce's father says she would be less successful if she were darker skinned', Andrew Trendell, www.nme.com, 6 February 2018

'I had been conditioned from childhood with eroticized rage',

> 'Beyoncé's father takes on "colorism": He dated mother because he thought she was white', Travis M. Andrews and Amber Ferguson, *Washington Post*, 5 February 2018

'White women and Black men have it both ways',

bell hooks, *Feminist Theory: From Margin to Center*, Pluto Press, 2000

Save the Last Dance, released 12 January 2001, Paramount Pictures

Sex and the City, Season 3 (2000), 'No Ifs, Ands or Butts'

'77 per cent of Nigerian women use skin-lightening products on a regular basis',

Pavitha Raol, 'Paying a high price for skin bleaching', www.un.org/africarenewal/magazine, April 2019 quoting WHO report, 2011

'In a conversation discussing Black love recorded in London in 1971',

James Baldwin & Nikki Giovanni, a conversation originally recorded for the PBS television series *SOUL!* Taped in London, November 1971 and later published as *A Dialogue* by J. B. Lippincott & Co., 1973

'Black women are five times more likely than white women to die in pregnancy',

'Why are so many black women still dying in childbirth?', Annabel Sowemino, *The Independent*, 20 August 2020

284

'Suicide is the largest killer of men under the age of 45',

www.menandboyscoalition.org.uk/
statistics, quoting ONS figures

'It's crazy that in 2019 we say, wow, this [a Black love
story] looks different',

'Director Barry Jenkins: I'm a black storyteller
telling a black story: that's progress', Bethany
Minelle, http://news.sky.com, 6 February 2019

7. THE UN-BLACKNESS OF QUEERNESS

'Kanye West summed up the homophobia',

'Revisit Kanye West railing against hip hop's
homophobia in 2005', Alexandra Pollard,
www.gigwise.com/news, 15 June 2016

'The only reason why our theological views are not
as foolish',

Daniel Kumler Flickinger, *History of the Origin,
Development and Condition of Missions Among
the Sherbro and Mendi Tribes in Western Africa*,
United Brethren Publishing House, 1885

'A study in 2016 measuring public attitudes to LGBTQ+ rights in Africa',

> 'The Personal and the Political: Attitudes to LGBTI People Around the World', The International Lesbian, Gay, Bisexual and Trans and Intersex Association, https://ilga.org, October 2016

'The question before the court is not whether the defendant's actions',

> 'US Court Dismisses Uganda LGBTI Case, but Affirms Rights', Graeme Reid, Human Rights Watch, www.hrw.org, 7 June 2017

'There is No Hierarchy of Oppression',

> Audre Lorde, From 'Homophobia and Education', New York: Council on Interracial Books for Children, 1983

8. PROPER BRITISH

'A study by the Migration Observatory at the University of Oxford in 2013',

> 'White Britons "will be minority" before 2070 says professor', *The Independent*, 4 May 2013

'Kim Kardashian who, after having a daughter called
North with the rapper Kanye West',

> 'Kim Kardashian vows to fight racism for baby
> North', Rachel Sigee, *Evening Standard*, 8 May 2018

'Will Smith: Racism Is Not Getting Worse, It's
Getting Filmed',

> www.hollywoodreporter.com, 3 August 2016

'The members go through life accepting the benefits of
membership',

> Noel Ignatiev, *How the Irish Became
> White*, London: Routledge, 2008

'I was taught to see racism only in individual acts of
meanness',

> Peggy McIntosh, 'White Privilege: Unpacking
> the Invisible Knapsack', *Peace and Freedom
> Magazine*, Philadelphia, PA, July 1989

'Legacy. What is a legacy? It's planting seeds in a garden
you never get to see',

> 'The World Was Wide Enough',
> *Hamilton: An American Musical*

9. A NEW NORMAL

'We fail to read the serial killer accurately',

Richard Tithecott, *Of Men and Monsters*: *Jeffrey Dahmer and the Construction of the Serial Killer*, University of Wisconsin Press, 1999

'Michelle Rodriguez, who appeared in the film *Widows* with the actor',

'Liam Neeson Can't Be Racist Because of How He Kisses, Says Michelle Rodriguez', Paul Chi, *Vanity Fair*, 7 February 2019

'Whoopi Goldberg said in his defence',

'Whoopi Goldberg defends Liam Neeson amid racism row: "He is not a bigot"', Jason Stolworthy, *The Independent*, 7 February 2019

'Looking beneath the history of one's country',

Isabel Wilkerson, 'The vitals of history', *Caste: The Origins of Our Discontents*, Penguin Random House, 2020, p.14

'BBC3 controller Fiona Campbell defended the show',

Abigail Gillibrand, *Metro*, 27 August 2020

'Until the lions have their own historians',

> 'Chinua Achebe, The Art of Fiction No. 139', the *Paris Review*, interview with Jerome Brooks, Winter, 1994

Aristotle, Book II of 'Nicomachean Ethics', 350 BCE

'Les Ferdinand, cousin of Rio and Anton, and director of football at QPR, defended his team discontinuing taking the knee',

> www.skysports.com/football/news – 22 September 2020

'We are all broken by something',

> Bryan Stevenson, *Just Mercy, a story of justice and redemption*, Scribe UK, 2015